THE QUEST FOR FREEDOM & DIGNITY

caste, conversion & cultural revolution

Other Books By Vishal Mangalwadi

THE QUEST FOR FREEDOM & DIGNITY

caste, conversion & cultural revolution

VISHAL MANGALWADI

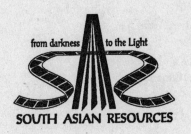

from darkness to the Light

SOUTH ASIAN RESOURCES

For current Information on the persecuted Church,
Please Contact:

The Voice of the Martyrs, Inc.

PO Box 443
Bartlesville, OK. 74005
(918)337-8015

THE QUEST FOR FREEDOM AND DIGNITY
Caste, Conversion and Cultural Revolution

© VISHAL MANGALWADI - Aug. 15, 2001

First Edition, Second Printing - February 2002

This SAR book is published by:
GLS Publishing

In partnership with:
Bibles for the World
P.O. Box 470
Colorado Springs, CO 80901
Telephone: (888) 38-BIBLE
Website: www.biblesfortheworld.com

To order in the USA and Canada, contact:
South Asian Resources
P.O. Box 453
Willernie, MN 55090
Telephone: (651) 426-4687
Fax: (651) 426-4694
E-mail: SAR@southasianresources.com
Website: www.VishalMangalwadi.com

Cover design by:
Vicky Naresh
E-mail: metroadliva@vsnl.net

Typeset by:
Horizon Printers and Publishers
E-mail: vishwas1@mantraonline.com

Printed in the United States of America
ISBN: 81-7820-063-5

All income from this book
is dedicated to the establishment of
a world-class institution of higher learning
for the oppressed in India
to fulfill the dream of
Mahatma Jotiba Phule
- pioneer of the Dalit revolution -
so that the
Light of the World
may continue to eradicate
all darkness from India.

To

Howard and Roberta Ahmanson,
Hugh and Nancy Maclellan,
and all Western Christians,
hated by some Indians
but loved by many more,
for their self-sacrificing generosity
to secure liberty and dignity
for victims of the
Hindu caste system.

The Quest for Freedom and Dignity

CONTENTS

Acknowledgements

The seeds of this book were sown in a prayer conference sponsored by South Asian Resources (SAR) on June 15-16, 2001. Ten days later Sunil Sardar and Dr. Rochunga Pudaite watered the seeds. Prayers, and the practical, financial and editorial assistance of many friends made it possible to bring this project to fruition in just six weeks.

I am grateful to Shri Ram Raj for contributing the Foreword, to Dr. Pudaite for his Afterword, and to Mr. Om Prakash Valmiki for his story, *Kahan Jaye Satish?*

My wife Ruth and I are temporarily in America to make a seven-hour documentary *The Book of the Millennium: How The Bible Changed Civilization.* Therefore, I needed special permission from the Managing Committee of SAR to undertake this project. They not only permitted me but also insisted on paying me, so that all the income from the book could go to a charitable cause in India. Thank you.

I am humbled that many Christians in America and England came forward to bear the financial responsibility for this project. This is not easy for us Indians to understand, because the story of a self-giving Messiah has not yet penetrated our Indian consciousness deeply enough. The astrological deities demand constant appeasement from their devotees. Therefore, even educated Indians suspect Western generosity to be something self-serving. For example, a Christian couple in America decided to adopt an unwanted, handicapped child from India. An Indian newspaper immediately interpreted it as an attempt to buy a baby to harvest organs for sale!

As a matter of fact, at this very moment there is a bill pending before the Indian Parliament to make foreign contributions harder to receive in India – particularly for a project like this one, which challenges Indian culture. There are powerful forces in India that would like to preserve the social status quo. That is what makes conversion a revolution and this book a threat. I hope the stories in this book will convince the reader that the oppressed in India need more, not less, international solidarity, for they are fighting not natural, but deeply entrenched human and diabolical forces.

Special thanks are due to Ivan Kostka for coordinating editing, proof-reading, cover design and page-making; to my daughter Anandit for translating Mr. Valimiki's story into English, and her other valuable suggestions; to David Hagen for invaluable research and editorial input; to Vicky Naresh for contributing the cover design; to Bruce Teichroew for pitching in during the critical last leg; to Brad Olson for taking over SAR office management and who, with Larry Landis and Cheryl Gardener, facilitated the effective use of the Internet to speed up the process of producing a book while making it increasingly an international collaborative enterprise.

Many friends made this project possible, but as usual, it is my dear wife Ruth who always ends up paying the emotional price of all my "very urgent" projects. Thank you, sweetheart!

V. M.

Foreword
by
Ram Raj, I. R. S.[1]

*National Chairman, All India Confederation of
SC/ST[2] Organisations
and Founder/President of the Lord Buddha Club*

India is known as a melting pot of many beliefs, cultures and superstitions. Westerners know it as a country of snake charmers and software engineers, acrobats and astrologers, Vedas and Yoga, the caste system and underdevelopment. India is all that and more. India's aboriginals created the Indus (or Harappan) civilization which was the largest and one of the greatest of the world's ancient civilizations. However, that great civilization was destroyed by the invading Aryans. Then the Aryans manipulated the Dravidians (native Indians, aboriginals or Dalits) into fighting each other. Domination was not easy for the Aryans, but was achieved by shrewd, unethical and immoral means. Since then, our society has deteriorated. That pattern of bondage for India's aboriginals continues to this day.

Almost all societies have undergone some kind of suppression or oppression. However, while many have overcome their problems, India remains stagnant. Why? First, the Aryans introduced myriad gods and goddesses into India. Then the Brahmins ("upper caste" Aryans) segmented society with legal sanctions in the name of God. India's whole society was stratified and divided into four major castes: Brahmins (the priestly caste) who claim to be born from the mouth of God,

Kshatriyas (the martial caste) supposedly from the arms of God, Vaishyas (the business caste) from God's belly, and the Shudras (the labour caste and "untouchables") from God's feet. This led to abject human conditions throughout India. An invisible civil war among the people became its permanent order.

The world is beginning to realize that caste is India's "apartheid." It has forced Dalits to live in separate colonies and do the most menial jobs. India's hidden inter-caste civil war is now spreading. In some states it is driving Dalits and Thakurs into separate villages. Revenge attacks are even burning down whole villages. High caste *senas* (armies) have massacred women and children. "Lower caste" vigilantes are striking back.[3]

Buddha tried his best to make our society humane, tolerant, peaceful, and friendly through his teachings, but through history this strife has continued. Similarly, St. Thomas, a disciple of Jesus Christ, traveled to India two thousand years ago and tried to share the way of freedom, but the Brahmins killed him. The noble attempts made to improve and humanize our society have been thwarted by the so-called "upper castes."

In this book Vishal Mangalwadi has successfully identified and traced the terrible wrongs that have befallen India. It becomes clear that the upper caste minority wants to maintain its theological and political hegemony, no matter what the consequences to our countrymen or to our country. Allowing that hegemony would permit them to continue reaping the economic benefits of the ongoing exploitation of the aboriginal majority of this country who have remained, in effect, slaves.

Reading through this book, I was often reminded of historical events that are so painful to every Indian patriot. In 327 BC Alexander the Great invaded India and his army was already at the River Jhelum (*Hydaspes*). On the other side of the river, a much bigger Indian army under King Porus awaited his attack. Seeing the size of the Indian army, for many days

Alexander could not gather the courage to attack. Then his curiosity was aroused by smoke rising from many different places in the Indian camp. He finally discovered that the Indian army did not dine and sleep together because of caste divisions in the soldiers' ranks. That information encouraged him to attack and win.

Such a consequence of our societal divisions was not an isolated incident in our history. It is commonly believed that Jaichand of Kanauj invited Mohammed of Ghur to defeat Prithviraj. Consequently, India was enslaved by the Turks from the early thirteenth century. Another Hindu king, Rana Sanga invited Babur, the Mongol who was then ruling Afghanistan, to attack India and to defeat Ibrahim Lodhi. Later Sanga himself, along with his allied Indian Muslim forces, was defeated by Babur in 1526, ushering in the long rule of the Mughals. With such a heritage of allying ourselves to foreign invaders for advantage over our domestic rivals, we made it easy for Robert Clive to defeat Indian armies and establish British rule with only a few hundred soldiers and bribery. But for the caste system, our motherland would probably not have been enslaved as it was for over a thousand years. It has often haunted my mind that if India had not been in bondage to social stratification, it could have become another amazing nation like the United States or Japan.

The problems the author describes are not happening in a vacuum. Rather, the victims also bear responsibility for their lot in life. Dr. B. R. Ambedkar tried his best to reform Hindu society, but it did not respond. Ultimately, he had to reject Hinduism for another faith. He chose to convert to Buddhism. Our system of reserving seats in educational institutions and in government positions for Dalits (oppressed aboriginals or "untouchables") was achieved through the Poona Pact of 1932. Dr. Ambedkar was not satisfied by this achievement. He knew that unless the caste system was abolished, Dalits would never regain their dignity. Today, many Dalits have entered politics and found government jobs through the Reservation System. But the greatest predicament is created when these Dalits continue to accept the caste system and their lowly place in it instead of what Dr. Ambedkar stood for. The world has witnessed many socio-cultural revolutions when those who suffered came forward to lead. So far, consciously or unconsciously, the victims of the caste system in India have largely looked to others to fight for and liberate them.

Recently, indiscriminate terrors and persecutions have been unleashed on Indian Christians because they are helping the untouchables and poor to get rid of the caste system, ignorance and poverty. The upper castes do not disdain Christ; they certainly hunger for the fruits of Christianity. Otherwise they would not have rushed to settle in developed Christian countries like the USA, nor would they have sent their children to Christian schools in India. The truth is that Christians and missionaries in India are opposed particularly when they try to help India's aboriginals, who were forced to become the "lower castes." In fact, all who try to help the downtrodden are opposed by the "upper castes." In the past, some of the British tried to help the downtrodden but faced stiff opposition from the "upper castes." Those thwarted attempts were abandoned to enjoy political power.

According to India's Home Ministry, Hindu gurus now bring far more "foreign contributions" into India than Christian missions. However, Hindus only attack Christian missions for "corrupting" the nation with "foreign contributions" because more of that money is used to serve the poor than the money brought in by Hindu gurus. Anything that is done to our country, including its division, is acceptable to the so-called "upper caste" - except the development and upliftment of the untouchables, backward communities, and minorities. This the upper castes do not tolerate.

Mr. Mangalwadi expertly diagnoses our Indian disease, evaluates alternative treatments and boldly prescribes a remedy. I, for one, feel Buddhism is an adequate philosophy to meet the challenges faced by the downtrodden. The author holds that Christianity is the solution. However, we both believe that the untouchables cannot escape their plight as long as they remain in the Hindu fold. What one cannot deny is that while three hundred and thirty million Hindu gods and goddesses have been worshipped for centuries, they have not improved the lot of a single enslaved Dalit. Yet, most of these sufferers continue to worship those impotent idols. Hinduism survives because of blind belief by the downtrodden. Even the best doctor cannot cure a patient if that patient refuses to follow the prescription. Now, it depends on our exploited people to respond to the prescription.

Hindu philosophy says that the world, which we perceive and experience, is unreal (*Maya*), and if reality exists then it is beyond this life and world. Accordingly, everyone should attempt to join this "reality." This is an invalid and untenable belief. If this religious proposition were true, or if the so-called "upper castes" actually believed this, then they should renounce this world and leave it for the Dalits to live in!

The fact is no effort to improve the situation of India's masses will succeed until the caste system is demolished. The caste system is blinding people's minds and blocking them from the freedoms of thought, faith, religion, and expression. The past is always justified and glorified, such as in the concept of *Ram rajya*.[4] The freedom for debate and argument, for thesis and antithesis, for new ideas and for progress, has never been allowed to most Indians. Despite our Constitution and the Reservation

System these freedoms are today denied in practice. Our freedoms are in danger of being destroyed even more in the future if the fascists of the Hindutva party are allowed to have their way.

Some readers may find Mangalwadi obsessed not only about the plight of untouchables but also with patriotism and nationalism. That can't be helped because he is a great patriot. The secret of development and progress in any country lies in the freedoms to choose and express faith and beliefs, thoughts and ideas. As long as most of our people can't exercise our constitutional freedoms, we will continue to be deprived of progress and advancement in our country.

True freedom is never granted by anyone on earth, be they "upper caste" or foreign invaders. Freedom has to be seized and used by people who understand that freedom is given equally to all human beings by God. However, freedom must be fought for, nurtured, invested in and maintained — otherwise it will be grabbed away from us once again by such "upper caste" power mongers who exploit our divisions.

In the final analysis it is up to us. We can choose to continue in slavery if we wish. Or we can choose to pay the cost and take hold of our God-given dignity and liberty.

New Delhi
August 15, 2001

Chapter One

What Enrages Dr. Maurya?*

The town fathers could have honoured Dr. Maurya. In 1984 he became the first *Shudra*[1] from a "Scheduled Caste" (SC)[2] to be appointed Medical Officer in the Government hospital in Louna.[3] His success was a social landmark: tangible evidence that a new India was being born where "untouchables" were free to develop their potential.

The elders could have been proud that Dr. Maurya had become a model, an inspiration to tens of thousands of lower caste children around Louna. The only role models these children previously had were ill-paid labourers, servants, cobblers, cleaners and rickshaw-pullers. Their social milieu conditioned them to believe that they were born to be slaves and servants to the upper castes. Dr. Maurya shattered that depressing paradigm. Therefore, he should have been used as an example to encourage demoralized children to unleash their intellectual and creative powers to contribute their best to "mother India." But the upper castes cared more for traditional Hindu culture than for their motherland. They refused

---

* This is a true story. The major events and discussions actually took place. However, the names of the places and some of the persons have been changed. The dialogues are creative recreations incorporating further reflection.

to accept Dr. Maurya, let alone respect him.

Dr. Maurya's appointment had brought to the surface a fundamental conflict between *Hindutva*[4] and patriotism. The upper castes sincerely want to be both – Hindu and patriotic. But the two involve opposing ideas of community organization. Hinduism fragments the nation into a hierarchy of unequal castes that aren't allowed to even eat together, let alone intermarry. Patriotism unites the nation on the principle of every citizen's equality before the law.

The leadership of Mahatma Gandhi's Congress party could have drawn political mileage from Dr. Maurya's appointment. They could have taken credit that "their" policy of reserving a quota of seats in medical colleges for the "untouchables" had begun to transform India. Arguably, the Reservation System[5] has opened up possibilities for men and women like Dr. Maurya, which were unimaginable five decades ago. Unfortunately however, the Reservation System does not liberate the upper castes from their bondage to the Caste System; they hated Dr. Maurya and the system that produced it.

On their first day in Louna, Dr. & Mrs. Maurya went out for a stroll. They needed to buy groceries and wanted to make friends in their new hometown. Mrs. Maurya had missed her afternoon tea, so they went into the best-looking restaurant and introduced themselves. They had expected the people in the neighbourhood to welcome an opportunity to become friends with their new doctor. A market economy should have prompted the restaurant owner to welcome a potential regular customer. But word about the social background of the new Medical Officer had already spread. The owner of the restaurant asked one of his servant boys to make their tea. The doctor had planned to tip the waiter with a sum befitting his occupational status in this small town. But the boy's demand stunned him.

This bare-chested, 13-year-old servant boy with dirty shorts announced, "No one in the restaurant would wash a cup used by a Shudra. Therefore you must wash your own cup." Dr. Maurya dashed his cup on the floor, threw a generous amount on the table and walked out. Everyone's smile seemed to say, "Good riddance."

A few months later a Muslim lawyer stopped me in the District Court, fifty kilometers from Louna. He began by complaining:

"Why hasn't anyone heard anything from you on Dr. Maurya's case?"

"What case? I've just arrived from New Delhi this morning."

They've thrown him in prison on a trumped up charge of rape. It's non-bailable. He'll rot in prison. His wife is expecting their first baby this month."

"I don't know Dr. Maurya and I've heard nothing." I had traveled all night and I did not have the energy to be patient with a man I barely knew, and who began the conversation with a complaint instead of a greeting. I rarely have time for gossip; on that day especially I needed to attend to some urgent matters, before returning to Delhi.

"Look!" the lawyer said, "no politician is going to meddle in this affair. Even I'm trying to get the BJP[6] ticket for the Vidhan Sabha.[7] I'll need upper caste support. You're the only one who could do something about this."

"I'm sorry! I don't know anything about the case and I'm here for only two days." I tried to end the conversation. But he wasn't taking my "no" for an answer.

"You've *got* to do something," he insisted. "Dr. Maurya's career has already been ruined."

By now my friend Rajan had joined us. He was a college student and an activist with the DS4 – *Dalit Shoshit Samaj Sangharsh Samiti* – a movement of Scheduled Caste youth, the predecessor of the Bahujan Samaj Party (BSP). Rajan confirmed that his people were agitated about Dr. Maurya's case and concurred with the lawyer that I needed to do something.

"Okay, tell me the story," I relented.

"Mummy came to Louna," the lawyer whispered. "The town elders told the honourable Member of Parliament for this area that they were not going to vote for her anymore. 'Why?' she asked. 'Because your party's policies have made this "untouchable" fellow a doctor,' they told her.

"Mummy summoned the doctor and began to verbally abuse him in public. The audience included the Medical Officer's subordinates.

"He said to the honourable Member of Parliament, 'Madam, if I have done something wrong, you can have me dismissed, suspended or transferred; but you can't insult me for no reason.'

"Mummy is not used to such arrogance, certainly not from 'untouchables.' Right in front of him, she said to her party-men, 'Teach him a lesson. I'll look after you.'"

"Wait a minute." I said, to the lawyer. "This is making no sense. Why would any sensible person, let alone a Congress MP, be upset because an 'untouchable' has become a doctor?"

"Are you dumb?" retorted the lawyer. "For centuries, upper caste men have stripped and raped lower caste women. Now this 'untouchable' fellow has acquired a position as a doctor to ask upper caste women to strip in front of him. The upper castes are furious. Mummy has realized that his appointment is the end of her political career. Perhaps of the Congress Raj itself."[8]

"Okay! Go on." I was getting interested. Of course, I didn't understand the lawyer's hidden agenda.[9] Nor did he realize that he was giving me my first glimpse into the gigantic socioreligious revolution that was reshaping India, beginning with its political landscape.

"The next evening," the lawyer continued, "the doctor and his brother were cooking dinner, because his wife had gone to her mother's home for her delivery. There was a knock at the door. As the doctor opened it three strangers, without saying a word, pulled him out and started beating him with hockey sticks.

"Behind them he saw a mob coming toward him. He got away, started his motorbike, and drove off to the police station. The mob caught his brother, beat him up and burnt all the household belongings. Then they went to the police station and demanded that the doctor be handed over to them.

"Coincidentally, the police officer on duty also happened to be a *Chamar*.[10] He refused to oblige the mob. They burned the doctor's bike and began hurling stones and abuses at the police:

> *Chamar daroga kya karega?*
> *Jute, chappal saf karega.*
> (What is the Chamar Inspector able to do?
> Nothing except clean our shoes and sandals.)

"The police inspector," the lawyer continued, "called the DM (District Magistrate) and the SP (Superintendent of Police). 'There's little we can do,' they replied. 'Mummy has spoken to us. Why don't you arrest the doctor on some charge and send him here to the district jail? That'll save his life.'

"The doctor was disguised in a police uniform and whisked away to the district headquarters. He thought he was being rescued but he ended up in prison, charged with raping a nurse. His brother was also arrested – for rioting and beating up people!

"The whole night a mob of about 200 men kept vigil around the police station. The next morning the crowd swelled to 2,000. When they discovered that the captive 'bird' had flown, mob fury took over. They went door-to-door in all the SC colonies, abusing, terrorizing and 'putting them all in their place.'"

"What did the Collector[11] do?" I inquired.

"He came later with the SP and asked Nurse Trivedi if she had been raped. 'No!' she said, 'The doctor patted me on my shoulder saying I was good with his patients. But I don't want him to touch me. He must know his place.'"

"So, why wasn't the rape charge dropped?"

"The case had already been registered on a complaint, signed probably by Mr. Trivedi. He had taken the lead in beating Dr. Maurya. Since the doctor had already been sent to jail, the case could not be retracted. It would have to be settled in court. Mrs. Trivedi would then have to choose between saving her husband or saving the doctor. Even if he can win the court case, the doctor will be financially wiped out. This is his first appointment. He doesn't have much money except his dowry."

"That *is* a sad story," I said to the lawyer, "but I don't see what I can do. Even if I knew what to do, I don't have the time. Let me think about it."

Having traveled all night, I didn't feel guilty about an afternoon siesta. When I woke up, I found myself thinking and praying about Dr. Maurya. One of the lawyer's statements began to perturb me: "No officer, no public figure, no journalist, will do anything about the doctor's plight."

Really?

Are we a society without conscience? Is there not one Hindu leader in the district who will stand up and say, "We are guilty"?

I found myself agreeing with the lawyer. I already knew that repentance was not an important value in our culture. If the doctor had indeed commended Mrs. Trivedi with a pat, then he was the "sinner" – as far as traditional culture was concerned. Eventually it was Adolf Hitler who helped me understand why a district with 1,200 towns and villages did not have one person who would stand up against such evil. Hitler said that "conscience" was a Jewish (Biblical) invention.[12] It did not fit in his Aryan worldview – nor does it fit the Hindu worldview.[13]

Still sleepy, I imagined a mob of 2,000 upper caste men descending on a lower caste colony with a dozen guns, loaded or unloaded. That would be sure to convince every "untouchable" child that becoming a police inspector or a doctor brings greater trouble than remaining a slave like his father. I began to realize that I was not being asked to intervene on behalf of an individual. At stake was the issue of whether or not I was committed to building a new India, where human dignity was valued, where lower castes were free.

A whole community had been silenced. Even a Muslim lawyer had been reduced to whispering. I might not be able to get Dr. Maurya out of prison and reinstated in his position, but what would prevent me from speaking: indifference, fear, or consent with the oppressors? Would not our silence condemn the oppressed to many more generations of slavery? Was I going to obey Jesus' command to love my neighbour as myself?[14]

In my half-sleep, I thought that I could probably get the story into the local papers if I took two hours that evening.

But it's an old story!

Well, then make it fresh: announce that the "untouchables" have planned a big protest rally the next day. That should intrigue the press. Who has ever heard of a protest rally in Louna, especially organized by the "untouchables"?

But could we really organize a rally with a few hours' notice?

What's the harm in trying? I thought to myself. In the morning I could send Rajan in a jeep with a team and a loudspeaker. He can take copies of the newspaper to convince folk that a protest rally is really happening. Everybody has heard of Dr. Maurya's case. Who knows, we might get a few thousand people. Even if they are too scared to come out on the streets, the oppressors would have already heard our protest via the press.

Just then Sachin and Rajan came to see if I was awake. That was more than perfect; it was providential. Sachin was a tall, handsome, Brahmin accountant and leader of an organization serving peasants. He had become a follower of Jesus Christ and a critic of the caste system. He was resourceful, savvy, and well connected – just the kind of support that Rajan needed to go into hostile and fearful villages and colonies to inspire confidence. Sachin also had a jeep!

They were both enthusiastic about the idea. I wrote out the press release. Rajan signed it as "Secretary, Ambedkar Mission" – a paper organization that I invented for that occasion. We went to a shop where we could get the story typed and the announcement stenciled.[15] Sachin drove Rajan to meet the editors of the local papers. They all knew Dr. Maurya's story anyway.

They had, of course, never heard of the "Ambedkar Mission." But they did know that the established "leaders" of the lower castes were Mummy's stooges and would not even dare whisper against her. Leadership for such a protest would have to come from new quarters. Rajan impressed them as intense and audacious. This unknown, "untouchable" young man had stepped forward to take on a Member of Parliament (MP). He had named her as the chief culprit and exposed the District Magistrate (DM) and the Superintendent of Police (SP) as subservient to unscrupulous politicians, not servants of the law! The fact that Sachin was driving the Secretary of the Ambedkar Mission was enough to make them think that the rally was really happening. The following morning the news story made the front page of three local papers.

It was Sunday. Sachin and Rajan were getting their team together while a loudspeaker was being tied to the jeep. With my Bible in hand, I was on my way to church. I was due to meet with a few more people and wind up my work in town. The plan was that I would come to Louna for the protest rally in the afternoon after they had got the crowd together and had set up the site. Following the rally I would head straight for the railway station.

However, the powers-that-be overruled my plans. Suddenly, in the middle of the road, just outside the church, I found myself sandwiched between two police jeeps. I was shocked. But the officer was extremely polite, "Sir, the SP Sahib wants to meet you, if you can please spare a few minutes."

I took his politeness at face value, even though I had learned that the police, as much as criminals, could be masters of deception. I soon found that he was merely trying to not create a scene in front of the church. Instead of taking me to the SP, he took me to the Sub-Divisional Magistrate. The SDM was curt and rude: "A curfew has been imposed in Louna; any gathering of five or more people is banned; the use of a public address system is outlawed; you are being detained because we do not want the peace and tranquility of the District disturbed."

Sachin and Rajan heard that I had been arrested just as they were leaving town. So with a jeep full of young men they tried to find me. But I had already been put behind bars, with nothing except my Bible. They went to my lawyer: a friend, a prominent politician, a leader of the socialist movement in our area, highly respected as a man of principles, in short, a local "Gandhi." Rajan invited him to be the main speaker at the protest rally. He smiled at Rajan's naiveté:

"I am a great admirer of Vishal and Ruth Mangalwadi, but no sane person would do what Vishal is doing in this case."

"What do you mean?" Rajan was puzzled.

"You tell me," asked the politician, "On one side there are 2,000 people; on the other side are 200 people. Whose side should I be on?"

Sachin and Rajan got the point: in a culture without moral absolutes, pragmatism will override principles. One must understand that in a relativistic world, principles are nothing more than a vocabulary of manipulation. Our socialist leader's rhetoric of social justice was only a means to get votes. He was no different than Mummy, whose party could, in its quest for power, equally promote and then destroy Dr. Maurya.

Sachin and Rajan decided that there had to be a first time for everything. They would lead the rally themselves, despite no experience of public speaking or, for that matter, of organizing and conducting public meetings. They drove the 50 kilometers to Louna, to discover that all entry points to the town had been barricaded by the police. They thought it would serve no purpose to get arrested on the outskirts of Louna. So they returned to the district headquarters, gathered together an audience of about 30 people, and had their first exercise in public protest. That gave the press some fodder for a further story. Two of the papers began a campaign for my release.

* * *

In prison I was amazed to find a hero's welcome. Within minutes the mystery was resolved: many inmates had read the morning papers with great excitement. The papers had not talked about me. In fact, the press did not even know that I was the "Ambedkar Mission." (I was already a controversial figure in the district and we had felt that the story might not be published if the editors knew that I – a controversial Christian – was the source.) The inmates were excited about the protest rally because Dr. Maurya had been kept in that very prison until a few days previously. He had won their sympathy. The inmates were electrified when they learnt that the author of the story they had been discussing for an hour or so had just arrived.

My identification with Dr. Maurya had been only intellectual. I did not even know him. The inmates had identified with him emotionally. Many of them had felt victimized by the same society and police. So, anyone campaigning for Dr. Maurya was championing them as well.

Prisoners, generally speaking, are serious thinkers. In the pre-modern world, prisons were dungeons. Criminals were given instant punishments: lashing, chopping off hands, slitting of noses, beheading, hanging or burning. Prisons were humanized and became "reformatories" in England as a result of vigorous campaigns by Christian groups such as the Quakers. Prisons ceased being dungeons and were made "cells," as in monasteries, to give lawbreakers time to think, meditate, pray and reform their lives. Now that the spirituality behind prisons has disappeared, inmates tend to come out of prisons worse than when they went in. Nevertheless prisons still turn men and women into thinkers. Every prisoner's case is discussed and debated at a depth much greater than in our law-courts. The prisoners consider not merely the legal dimensions of their cases, but also the human and, at times, even the philosophical aspects. A prisoner thinks, because he/she has little else to do. That Sunday the prison turned into a discussion chamber for my case.

All prisoners agreed that the Member of Parliament and law enforcement officers had abused the law in order to persecute first Dr. Maurya and then me. By arresting me they had violated my fundamental rights. But were they, thereby, law-breakers: criminals?

Several narrated their own experiences of the rulers' disregard for law. Some prisoners, however, were unwilling to call rulers "criminals." The dissenters agreed that the rulers' claim to uphold the "rule-of-law" was a sham, and that our nation was degenerating because the sanctity of law was a foreign concept.

Indian culture did have a "sacred" law, but that law of Manu[16] justified untouchability, oppression of women and any means needed to retain the social hierarchy. The "secular" law, that advocated equality, was human law. How could the ruling elites, that made secular law, be under that law? What mattered ultimately, the dissenters contended, was power, not law. In spite of breaking the law the rulers were not "criminals," because the rulers had the power. No one is a "criminal" unless convicted by a court.

Some dissenters went as far as to argue that even after one is convicted by a court, he/she is not a criminal if he/she wins an election and becomes a minister. "It is all about power," was their settled conviction. Many prisoners said they had decided to join a political party after they came out of prison.

The discussion had gone in circles for some time when Ghasiram, a low caste man from the Teli (oil makers) caste, interrupted, asking for my opinion.

"Does my liberty," I asked him, "to travel to Louna, to organize a rally and express my opinion come from God, or is my freedom a gift from our rulers? If my 'fundamental' rights are nothing but a gift from human rulers, then, of course, they have the right to withdraw their gift. But what if my freedom of conscience is a gift from our Creator?"

"In that case," grasped Ghasiram, "the rulers should be *guardians* of your freedom."

"What would you say, I continued, if there is a God and He made all human beings to be his children – equal, like real brothers and sisters? What if human equality is God's desire and command, and the 'secular' law only reflects God's law?"

"If equality is God's law," mused Ghasiram, "then the persecutors of Dr. Maurya are sinners whether or not a court is able to convict them."

"That," I concurred, "is the secret behind the principle of the 'rule-of-law.' If there is no God, and if He has not revealed His will to us, then we are forever condemned to be ruled by the whims of rulers. One day they will promote freedom for me, and equality for a Dr. Maurya. The next day they would throw us in prison if our assertion of our liberty or dignity becomes too inconvenient for them. Freedom, democracy, and rule of law are implied in or precluded by a culture's belief-system."

"Do you believe in God?" Ghasiram asked me pointedly.

"Yes, I came to this district to serve Him."

"I have often heard about you," Arun Vajpayee butted into our conversation abruptly, "from Sharmaji[17] and others. They say that you are a very religious person, a good missionary. But they can't understand your motives. Why should a religious person like you meddle in political matters?"

"What does the word 'Messiah' mean to you?" I asked him.

"Liberator! A champion of the oppressed," he replied.

"Exactly! 'Christ' is the Greek word for Messiah. It means one who is anointed by God to liberate the oppressed. It is one of the titles for the Lord Jesus, because he declared:

> 'The Spirit of the Lord is on me,
>   because he has anointed me
>   to preach good news to the poor.
> He has sent me to proclaim freedom
>   for the prisoners
>   and recovery of sight to the blind,
>   to release the oppressed,
>   to proclaim the year of the Lord's favor.'[18]

"But wasn't Jesus a religious teacher?" Vajpayee was puzzled.

"He was. But Jesus quoted that passage from the Jewish prophet Isaiah, who had lived about seven hundred years before Christ. In Isaiah's day the Jews thought that being religious was a matter of observing rituals, offering sacrifices to God, praying and fasting. Some thought that God could be appeased by fasting and offering sacrifices, while they carried on with their usual corruption, oppression and injustice. Isaiah corrected this misunderstanding. He declared that God was morally pure and wanted justice, righteousness and compassion, not bribes. He prophesied:

> 'Is not this the kind of fasting that I have chosen:
>   to loose the chains of injustice
>   and untie the cords of the yoke,
>   to set the oppressed free
>   and break every yoke?

Is it not to share your food with the hungry
    and to provide the poor wanderer with shelter –
    when you see the naked, to clothe him,
    and not to turn away from your own flesh
    and blood?
Then your light will break forth like the dawn,
    and your healing will quickly appear . . .
If you do away with the yoke of oppression,
    with the pointing finger and malicious talk,
    and if you spend yourselves in behalf of the hungry
    and satisfy the needs of the oppressed,
    then your light will rise in the darkness,
    and your night will become like the noonday.
The Lord will guide you always;
    he will satisfy your needs in a sun-scorched land
    and will strengthen your frame.
You will be like a well-watered garden,
    like a spring whose waters never fail.
    Your people will rebuild the ancient ruins
    and will raise up age-old foundations;
    you will be called Repairer of Broken Walls,
    Restorer of Streets with Dwellings.'"[19]

"What," I asked Vajpayee, "according to Isaiah, constitutes true spirituality?"

"Liberating the oppressed!" He answered without hesitation.

"What yoke must we break to set the oppressed, like Dr. Maurya, free?"

"Caste!" exclaimed Ghasiram.

"I've heard Christian preachers before," said Vajpayee, "especially in the Christian Hospital, but I've never heard anyone say that Christianity had anything to say on social issues like caste."

To be a Christian, I explained, means to be a follower

of the Lord Jesus Christ. If you read his story in any of the four Gospel narratives in the Bible you will find that his society hated him because he intentionally defied their rules regarding untouchability. Casteism or racism is not a peculiarly Hindu problem. All human beings are sinners and find it hard to love their neighbours as themselves. The Jews, for example, did not mix with the half-breed Samaritans. Jesus shocked them by asking a Samaritan woman at a well to give him some water to drink.[20] The Jews also treated tax collectors,[21] lepers,[22] and non-Jewish "gentiles"[23] as "untouchables." But Jesus associated with them, ate with them and publicly touched them — yes, he *touched* the lepers and healed them; that is why his followers started all these leprosy asylums in India. Jesus taught that God desires mercy, not sacrifices or ceremonial purity. To be truly godly we need to love even our enemies, besides the untouchables, because they are our neighbours.[24]

"But how can the yoke of caste be broken?" asked Ghasiram.

The conversation moved on to the subject of the Reservation System. It had been debated thoroughly when Dr. Maurya was in prison. The inmates were divided.

The upper caste prisoners had concluded that one could not take the benefit of being "low caste" without also taking the stigma of being low caste. The Reservation System enabled Maurya to become a doctor because he was an "untouchable." How could he benefit from being born an "untouchable," and demand that he should be treated as an equal? If he were not an "untouchable," he would not have been admitted to Medical School and so could not have become a doctor! A Reservation System built on the assumption of inequality would necessarily reinforce inequality. It could not be used to destroy its own assumptions.

The lower caste prisoners believed the Reservation System had benefited hundreds of thousands of lower caste families; therefore, it should be continued even though it has failed as an instrument of social transformation. In fact, Dr. Maurya's case showed that Reservations reinforce caste prejudices.

The inmates had had several rounds of debates and reached a stalemate. They wanted to know if I had any fresh insights. I shared the following thoughts with them.

The problem with the caste system and the Reservation System is that they are both attempts at social engineering. Social engineering is the opposite of social transformation. The caste system favors the upper castes, so they like it. The Reservation System benefits the lower castes; therefore many cling to it. The result is a perpetuation of the status quo.

Casteism is one of history's first grand attempts to create a social utopia via social engineering. It turned into a monstrosity like all attempts at social engineering do. It became possibly the single greatest hindrance to India's progress. The caste system is evil for many reasons: one of them is that it stifles citizens' growth by taking away their freedom to do what they are good at and motivated to do.

The Reservation System is also social engineering on a smaller scale, so its consequences are not as bad as those of the caste system. Reservation was a secular method of correcting our society's social ills. Its problem is that it makes the State the saviour. It does help some people, but it fails to address root issues — our false beliefs and lack of love for one another — thus it creates fresh problems.

Today the upper castes, opposed to reservations, are moving their support from the Congress party to the BJP. But can any democratic party do away with the Reservation System? Not as long as the lower castes have votes. Sooner or later the upper castes will have to choose between democracy and the idea of equality on the one hand and the traditional Hindu culture that promotes social hierarchy on the other. The defenders of Hindu culture will condemn democracy as an "alien political system," a source of corruption, indiscipline and mediocrity.

Throwing me into prison simply because I opposed what they did to Dr. Maurya was anything but democracy. The upper castes in Louna must have been pleased I was in jail. Some of them may want open dictatorship, because then the lower castes would have no civilized means of redressing the ills of our society. Dictatorship would eventually lead to a bloodbath, greater animosity, and to our nation's disintegration.

"If social engineering is a hopeless idea, then how does one transform a society?" someone asked.

"At the time of the Lord Jesus, Israel was a colony of Rome. The Jews were looking for a messiah who would liberate them from their slavery. Many followed Jesus in the hope that he might be their liberator. Jesus said to these followers,

'If you hold to my teaching, you really are my disciples. Then you will know the truth, and the truth will set you free.'[25]

"At its source slavery begins in our minds, in what we choose to believe. False ideas enslave, truth liberates. Mahatma Jotiba Phule, the nineteenth century pioneer of the Dalit revolt in India called his society *Satya Shodhak Samaj* (Truth Seeker's Society) because he understood what the Lord Jesus was saying. Mahatma Phule knew that nations like England were not reformed by the state's attempts at social engineering. What enabled them to abolish slavery, the slave trade, and serfdom, and become prosperous democracies? Mahatma Phule knew that

Europe's transformation began with reformers-cum-Bible translators like Martin Luther and William Tyndale who committed themselves to finding and following truth. What India needs is a similar intellectual, moral and spiritual reformation.

"Casteism is enslaving because it rests on a lie that God created human beings unequal. We are different from each other because we are unique, just as each child in a family is unique and different. Being different in our aptitudes, abilities, interests, and motivations does not make us unequal. Just as wise and sensitive parents invest more of their love, affection, time and resources in a child who is weak, we too must invest in caring for those who need greater support.

"We may indeed need to 'reserve' special privileges for our weaker brothers and sisters. But our primary need is not reservation. It is truth – a change in our perspective – that would enable us to perceive our neighbours as our brothers – not high or low caste. Becoming a doctor did not add to Dr. Maurya's dignity, because the citizens of Louna continued to see him through the lens of a false worldview. Without shattering the false belief system that enslaved him, he cannot have the liberty to be a doctor with dignity.

"But right beliefs are inadequate. We are sinners: we envy other people's success, we are jealous, we hate. We need a transformation of our hearts: the ability to support our competitors' efforts and applaud their success. The Lord Jesus knew that we are enslaved not merely by false ideas but also by sin. Therefore he continued,

> '. . . everyone who sins is a slave to sin. . . . So if the Son sets you free, you will be free indeed.'"[26]

* * *

The prison conversation went on for four days until I was released. Ghasiram, who was on trial for murder, was released a few months later. Along with another friend he joined our community to study the Bible and became a follower of Christ.

Eventually Ghasiram, Rajan, and I met with Dr. Maurya. The District Court had sentenced him to ten years rigorous imprisonment and his brother to two years. Unable to fight, he had negotiated a settlement with his oppressors that enabled him to appeal in the High Court. Now he was out on bail, living thirty kilometres from Louna in a rented apartment. He was very grateful to me but traumatized by the thought that evil had triumphed. He could not look his "wicked" subordinates in the eye. They held him in utter contempt. He felt he had no option but to move out of the state and start a private practice in a town where few knew him.

Public humiliation and victimization by such blatant injustice had shattered Dr. Maurya's hopes for India, as well as his personal dreams. There were times, he said, when his "blood boiled" with anger and hatred. He wanted nothing but revenge. In sober moments he was resigned to his fate. He couldn't afford to go back to jail as he had a wife and a new baby to bring up. So while he could not forgive his oppressors, he had to make peace with them! In moments of helplessness he found himself agreeing with Gautam Buddha's first Noble Truth: "*Life is suffering.*"

But then he questioned it: Should a doctor's life be suffering? Can't India be so transformed that a doctor can practice his profession with self-respect?

At times he felt that Buddha was right: that *desire* – his desire for liberty and dignity – was the source of his suffering. But then, how were the lower castes to rise if they gave up their desire for their advancement?

"Please don't give up your desire and your hope," I pleaded with Dr. Maurya. The Lord Jesus' disciples were also overwhelmed by the power of evil when they saw their Lord hanging on the cross; publicly humiliated, brutally tortured and killed. He had told them that they were living in the kingdom of Satan. A statement like that sounds nothing more than a religious cliché, until you actually challenge Satan's kingdom and face evil's fury. The disciples thought that their quest for liberty was finished when Jesus was nailed on the cross. But from that very cross Jesus declared that it was the kingdom of Satan that was finished. Jesus displayed the triumph of goodness over evil, when on the cross he prayed for his torturers, "Father, forgive them for they know not what they do."

I explained to Dr. Maurya that his oppressors were like the Lord Jesus' tormentors whose spiritual blindness prevented them from seeing what they were doing. Nevertheless, for his inner peace and healing, as well as for building a strong community in India, Dr. Maurya needed to forgive them. Obviously he could not do so in his own strength. He needed God's grace in his heart. If he opened his heart, Jesus would come into his life and give him his own divine life that enabled him to forgive his persecutors on the cross. It would be easier for Dr. Maurya to forgive those who had sinned against him, once he acknowledged that he too was a sinner, in need of divine forgiveness. Bringing forgiveness and reconciliation between man and God, and between man and man was the chief purpose of Christ's sacrifice on the cross.

Jesus' death and resurrection inaugurated a new kingdom – the kingdom of love.[27] The Lord Jesus has the power to transform Brahminism's kingdom of castes and to give us love for those who hate us. Three days after his death, God raised Jesus from the dead, demonstrating that God, not evil, was the ultimate power in this universe. The Reservation System has obviously failed as a means of our deliverance. But, before you resign yourself to your *karma*, please explore the power of Christ's resurrection: God's power to deliver us from evil.

Chapter Two

Manju's Honour*

Manju was most excited by her results in the Board examination. Now she didn't have to get married!

She was the first SC[1] girl in Baragaon to pass High School,[2] and the only student in her village school to pass with a First Class.[3] She had scored a distinction[4] in Mathematics – a subject other girls avoided. Having worked and hoped for these results, she had extracted a promise from her parents that if she got a First Class they would allow her to continue her studies without the interruption of marriage.

The result was a mix of emotions for Dhaniram. He was proud of Manju and madly in love with her. But he had just turned 18, and become eligible for a bank loan to buy an auto-rickshaw. He wanted to marry Manju and take her to live in the neighbouring town. Thanks to Vermaji, the bank manager, Dhaniram would own the very first auto-rickshaw in town.

Like them, Vermaji was also a *Chamar;*[5] he knew what it meant to struggle in life. Vermaji was impressed by Dhaniram's father. He had begun as a rickshaw puller; over time bought his own rickshaw and then, with Vermaji's help, he bought five more rickshaws and a pushcart. Young men from his village

---

* This treatment for a film script is a work of fiction. All the characters are fictitious; any resemblance to persons living or dead is coincidental.

drove his rickshaws, while he used the pushcart to sell peanuts.

Dhaniram had failed the Board exams the previous year. Thanks to Manju's coaching he had managed to pass this year, albeit with a third division. Recognizing that he was not good academically he had decided to focus on expanding his father's transportation business, beginning with an auto-rickshaw.

Manju liked Dhaniram, but she agreed with the Principal of her school that her people needed to delay marriage and devote their energies to self-development before rearing families. Dhaniram was consoled by her reminder that *Dhiraj ka phal meetha hota hai.*[6]

During the next two years Manju became an exemplary student in Baragaon, while some underemployed SC, OBC,[7] and Muslim youth in town began to gather around Dhaniram. They loved free rides on his auto-rickshaw. He was often hired to take patients from the hospital back to their villages, and haul *bidis*[8] from the neighbouring villages into town. Whenever he could, he would take one or two boys to keep him company and help with loading and unloading. Soon a network of relationships had begun to build up. Mahmud Miyan, the bidi contractor, became his single biggest customer.

Two years did not take as long as Dhaniram had feared. The wedding was a grand affair, although being a Chamar, he was not allowed to ride on a horse. However, some village elders perceived the Shudra's struggle for self-development as "disruptive of social order." Toward the end of the ceremony two gun-carrying *thakurs*[9] arrived at the wedding site with a present – a stainless steel *thali*[10] – from Raja Shankar Singh, the village chief. Manju's family was touched by the gesture. The couriers whispered to Manju's father that the elders were concerned about the young people forgetting the traditional *shishtachar.*[11] They suggested that because Manju was leaving the village the next morning, she ought to go to the *haveli*[12] and pay due respects to the Raja Sahib. She would thus uphold the honour of the village.

Two of Manju's aunts and some friends of Dhaniram escorted the couple to the haveli, while the parents said goodbyes to guests who were returning to neighbouring villages and organized cots and mats for those who had to spend the night with them.

Armed thakurs stopped the couple's escorts outside the courtyard, "Raja Sahib does not like crowds at night," they said. "If the couple want his blessings, they can go inside the courtyard by themselves."

Dhaniram was stopped at the haveli's giant entrance. "You don't belong to our village; your father migrated to the town years ago. Manju is the daughter of the village, so if she wants to she could touch Raja Sahib's feet."

As Manju stepped into the haveli, the guards escorted Dhaniram out of the courtyard, "Go, drink and sleep now," they said. "In any case, you are not supposed to see her before the *bidai*."[13]

"I'll wait for my wife," Dhaniram announced with the self-respect of a town-dweller.

Tarrak . . . a powerful slap from one of the armed men made Dhaniram's head spin. "Do you want to f... her right away? She is not your wife yet. She is still the daughter of our village. She will be yours only after the bidai. Tonight she has to be taught to uphold the honour of our village. They don't teach culture in schools. You Chamars are becoming too big for your boots."

Dhaniram's friends were terrified of the guns pointed at them. They dragged him away as he began abusing the chief in the foulest language he knew. The armed thakurs matched his language as they warned that if anyone returned that night, they would shoot first and ask questions later.

Dhaniram was still cursing when they returned to Manju's family. "Where is Manju?" asked her worried father. Instead of answering, Dhaniram started his auto-rickshaw and headed to the road. Three of his friends managed to jump in; one was left behind, warning the family not to go back to the haveli without arms. "Wait for Dhaniram," he advised, "maybe he has a plan. He might bring the police, or perhaps Mahmud Miyan's men."

Mahmud Miyan gave Dhaniram a glass of country liquor, sat him down, and taught him a lesson: "We must strike when the time comes, not in a rage. Tonight the Raja is armed and waiting for you. Trust me, we'll get him. He is my biggest headache. He gets the contract for *tendu* leaves from the Forest Department but I do all the work. If he were not there I would get the contract and make four times more from the work that I already do. Have patience. We'll come up with a plan."

Divested of her dignity and virginity Manju returned home at 3 a.m. The guests began to disappear before sunrise, in case Dhaniram returned with *goondas*[14] from the town. They had come to celebrate, not fight. In any case, there was no bidai as Dhaniram woke up only at noon and with a hangover. In the evening, Manju's father was told that his son-in-law would take his daughter to her new home only after avenging his humiliation.

One evening, about a month later, Raja Shankar Singh heard that someone was stealing his stock of tendu leaves from the jungle 20 miles from his village. He slung his rifle on his back, got on his motorbike with a bodyguard behind him. The report turned out to be baseless. There was no trace of anyone having been around. The stock was lying exactly as it had been left the previous day for the driver of the Forest Department to bring the Department's truck on a private trip and haul it to Shankar

Singh's warehouse for a small tip.

On his way back Raja Sahib was relaxed but drove fast as it was beginning to get dark. Suddenly his neck struck a stainless steel wire tied across the road between two trees. The motorcycle under him roared on for several yards, and finally slammed to a halt as it crashed into some rocks. The next morning two bodies were found on the rocks, their skulls cracked open. The motorcycle was a twisted heap of metal. It seemed to have been a gruesome accident because their rifles, wallets and watches were intact.

Within a week Mahmud Miyan had paid off Dhaniram's auto-rickshaw loan and helped him with the down payment for a brand new jeep. Vermaji, the bank manager, was as helpful as ever. Manju became the first passenger to drive in the new jeep to her husband's home.

The jeep brought much business and many new friends. Dhaniram used his Scheduled Caste status to obtain a fishing contract from the Fisheries Department. The *Dheemers*[15] caught the fish on his license and his jeep hauled them to the railway station. The business grew to the extent he was supplying fish as far away as Calcutta. His need to drive through the jungles required him to also obtain a gun license. During the day the jeep did regular business, at nights it began to be used for hunting and drinking parties. Dhaniram began dreaming of buying more jeeps and then a truck.

Some SC college students in town, however, had other plans for Dhaniram. They had become involved with a new political party that promised to make Shudras the new rulers of India. The party taught that 3,000 years ago the Aryans had invaded India from across the border, colonized her original inhabitants and made them "untouchables." Now, if they – the rightful owners of India – wanted to they could retake the Government of India as their heritage, in a bloodless, democratic revolution, because they were still the majority. These students wanted Dhaniram to become their local patron. If he helped them with a donation and his jeep, they would go to all the neighbouring villages and towns, educating and uniting the victims of the "Aryan conspiracy." "When the next election comes," they told Dhaniram, "we want you to run for Parliament on our party's ticket."

At first Dhaniram took them to be naïve idealists. But soon he began to hear that national newspapers had begun writing about this party, which was storming the political citadels, which had been the monopoly of the upper castes until then. The students persisted in their appeals, and Mahmud Miyan and Vermaji encouraged Dhaniram to help them out. Some friends from a neighbouring state had visited Vermaji, indoctrinated him, and taken him to witness the new life the party had breathed into the lower castes, who – until then – had lived like demoralized slaves.

A few months later the president of the new party came to address a rally in a neighbouring district. The students persuaded Dhaniram to come with them to listen to their "Sahib." The rally became a turning point. Dhaniram also accepted the Sahib as his "Messiah" and threw his wholehearted support behind the students. Soon he was going out with them to attend, and then to speak at, their meetings. His network of relationships came in handy and he established the local unit of the party within a few months.

Manju was pleased that his time was no longer spent with his drinking and hunting partners. Yet she was finding it hard to bring up the children by herself and also work on her Ph.D. Politics had become a new addiction for Dhaniram. His "mission" overruled her pleas for him to spend time with the family. He was keeping the promise he had made to her that he would allow her to complete her Ph.D. But he had made no promise to baby-sit. That was "a woman's job."

The earnestness of the college students that surrounded Dhaniram impressed Manju. She also liked their ideology. Nevertheless, they were her new rivals for his time and attention. They had some meeting or the other planned for Dhaniram every evening and every weekend.

Manju agreed that her addiction to education was not necessarily nobler than his addiction to politics. Both required sacrificing family time. But then, who knows, one day her husband might actually become an MP.[16] Then she would benefit too.

Parliamentary elections were a few months away when Vermaji got a phone call from Delhi that the Sahib had agreed to come to their town for a public rally. His condition was that the local unit of the party must organize a crowd of at least 10,000 people and honour him with a purse of Rs.20,000. Dhaniram and Mahmud Miyan took up the challenge. They decided to mobilize a crowd of 20,000 and present a purse of Rs.50,000, underwriting any shortfall from the local collection. This, they believed, would convince Sahib that the party could win their seat. If he were convinced he would pay more attention to their district and during the election might reinvest their contribution to win this seat.

The big day came; it was a huge success! Sahib's speech won them many converts. He emphasized the need to educate, organize, and agitate in order to recover the human dignity that the oppressed had lost 3,000 years ago.

Sahib was told that Dhaniram had worked day and night to

make the rally a success and that his wife was a brilliant student. Manju cooked and brought the dinner to the guesthouse for Sahib and his entourage. She greeted him respectfully and sat down on a sofa. Vermaji and Mahmud Miyan were the next to arrive. They touched Sahib's feet and sat down on the floor, although the guestroom had more sofas and chairs. Other visitors soon started pouring in. They would all touch Sahib's feet and sit down on the floor. Manju began to feel awkward. No one had told her that party members were not supposed to sit on chairs in Sahib's presence. She got up and went into the kitchen to heat the food.

Raja Shankar Singh was the last man at whose feet Manju had bowed. Ever since then she had agreed with the Lohiaites[17] that to bow at someone's feet was to violate one's own dignity. Now in the Sahib's chamber Manju found herself to be the "odd one out." She did not know whether to revere the Sahib or to affirm her dignity and human equality.

When she came back to serve dinner, she found Sahib to be a gentleman. He went out of his way to put her at ease. During dinner he talked more to her about her Ph.D. than to Dhaniram about his business and politics. He seemed especially gentle toward her, singling her out for special attention.

Later, just as Dhaniram and Manju were getting ready to leave in their jeep, Jeevan Babu, Sahib's assistant, came up to them and took Dhaniram aside. Dhaniram returned several minutes later with a gleam in his eyes. He started the jeep, moved a few feet and blurted out, "Sahib has decided to give me the Lok Sabha[18] ticket. But he wants you to come back after the others are gone and spend the night with him."

"What?" Manju was shocked.

"Yes! Jeevan Babu said that the Sahib is really impressed with you."

"What does that mean? Does he sleep with every woman that 'impresses' him?"

"But he is our President. We have to respect him."

"Are you crazy? What about *our* respect?"

"Manju, this is for *my* sake. Jeevan Babu said that this is how Sahib 'tests' how dedicated his followers are to his mission."

"How, then, is your Sahib different than Raja Shankar Singh? He was also 'guarding the honour of our village' when he dishonoured me. Are you going to sell my honour in order to honour another creep? Have you dedicated yourself to his mission or surrendered your self-respect at his feet?"

Dhaniram's pride was stung. He had barely slept for days and he couldn't take her rebuke.

"Shut up!" he screamed. "I don't want to hear your lecture."

There was a stony silence the rest of the way. At home he got drunk and went off to sleep. She stayed up crying.

The election date drew near. Dhaniram had spent tons of personal money in building up the party besides sacrificing business interests and family life. He was sure he was going to get the Lok Sabha ticket. Sahib, however, gave the ticket to Mahmud Miyan "because the party needed to woo the Muslim voters."

Dhaniram complained. Jeevan Babu reminded him of the night when he had failed to honour Sahib. "You didn't give him what he asked for; how can you now expect to get what you ask for?"

Disillusioned, Dhaniram took to drinking and hunting again. His relationship with Manju deteriorated. He was rarely at home; when he was, he was irritable and short-tempered. Once or twice Manju stood up for her rights. In his drunkenness he beat her, blaming her for destroying his political career. Once he went to the extent of saying that he thought Shankar Singh was right: Modern women needed to be taught the time-honored etiquette of submission to men; her education had made her too arrogant.

Manju cried her heart out to Shanti, who had come to their town from Andhra Pradesh with her husband David. Shanti wanted to do a B.A. in Hindi and was taking lessons from Manju. With Manju's permission, Shanti prayed with her that the Lord would fill Manju's heart with peace and give her strength to face the trials she was going through, because "he had come into this world to bear our sin and suffering."

The prayer made no sense to Manju. She thought it strange that Shanti should talk to God as though he was an easily accessible father to her.

The home situation got worse. Dhaniram complained that education, not he, had always been Manju's first love. Why was her Ph.D. taking forever? What did she want to do with it? Why should she want to work with other men when she could help him expand his business?

Shanti invited her to talk to her husband. Manju asked David, had she been wrong in not honouring the Sahib?

They talked for a couple of hours. She was moved when David, in order to answer her question, told her the story of the Messiah, the anointed leader who became a servant to his disciples. David said that after the disciples had walked on a dusty road and gathered together for a ceremonial feast, the Messiah got up from the table, took off his outer garments, took a basin of water and began washing his disciples' feet. Then he said to his disciples that among the gentiles their rulers lorded it over them, but the new kingdom that he was inaugurating would be different. In his kingdom, whoever wanted to be leader must become a servant to others. He himself had come, not to be served, but to serve and give his life so that others might be free and live with dignity.[19]

David explained one of the sources of democracy that Dhaniram's Dalit "Messiah" was using to liberate the oppressed. The democratic revolution in England was a culmination of a spiritual revolution that began with the Lord Jesus washing his disciples' feet. This revolution deprived the kings of England of their power and it increased the servants' power to a point that the "First Servant" (the Prime Minister) became the most important office; and, he ruled, not with the help of soldiers, but with a battalion of "civil servants."

"Do you mean to say," Manju thought out loud, "that a political revolution won't change much in our nation without a spiritual revolution?"

"Do you really believe," David asked, "that someone who demands that his followers sit at his feet and surrender their wives to him, would restore their dignity to them?"

Manju became anxious to finish her doctorate. She sensed that it would become an increasingly contentious issue in their marriage. Professor Shreevastav, her guide, however, was always too busy for her. He would ask her to meet him in his room after college hours; he would talk about her children, her clothes and her jewelry, but not about her thesis. Each time she would press him, the most he would do was give her a title or an author to read. He had not been able to read her draft chapters, he would explain, because of all the other responsibilities that had been thrust upon him by the University. He barely had time to read the minutes of the committees he had been elected to.

Manju realized that he was making excuses. He did have time to play cards with his colleagues. He seemed to have watched every new movie from Bollywood[20] as well as Hollywood.

Panditji, the department's peon,[21] resolved Manju's puzzle.

"Even the gods have to be appeased," he said, "if you want their blessings."

"What do you mean?"

"No one gets a Ph.D. here," said the old man, "by head-knowledge alone. You have to also learn some *shishtachar.*"[22]

"*Bhartiya bhrashtachar,*[23] you mean?!" Manju snapped in rage. The memories of her wedding night rushed back to enrage her.

"What's wrong with sleeping with someone who dreams of you every night? You'll get not only your Ph.D., but also a job and quick promotions. In any case, no one is forcing you to hurry up your thesis. You can take as long as you like."

Manju cried all the way back home. Dhaniram had already left for the night with his hunting partner. She tossed and turned in her bed the whole night, weighing her options. Could she complain to the University without any proof? How might Dhaniram react? By the morning she was more confused than she had been at night. She thought she now understood why other students who began their theses after her had managed to complete them before her.

But did Professor Shreevastav really dream of her every night? That would be more than Dhaniram did. There was little intimacy between them now. What exactly was wrong if she slept with him ... just once? Who knew what Dhaniram did during those drinking and hunting parties? Wasn't she entitled to some fun in life?

Manju didn't go to the library the following day. When she next saw the professor, he told her that the UGC[24] had invited him to read a paper at a seminar in New Delhi. The Assistant Professor was not able to join him; the seminar would give her an opportunity to make key national and international contacts in her field. So if she wanted to come along, all expenses would be paid for by the UGC.

Manju had learnt the consequences of "dishonouring" those who had power. The seminar was tempting. She needed a change. Dhaniram could not possibly object to a professional trip. But she also knew why the opportunity was being offered to her rather than to others in the department.

"Why not? What's wrong?" was one voice in her heart.

"So what was wrong with Dhaniram's Sahib's invitation?" asked another voice.

Manju shared her moral dilemma with Shanti and David. Shanti had told her that they prayed for her everyday. "Should a student get a degree," asked David, "on the merit of his work or bribes?"

"I see!"

"This culture of bribery will never allow our democracy to become a meritocracy," continued David. "It doesn't matter which caste rules over us. Without a moral and spiritual regeneration, India will forever remain mediocre. Should your Ph.D. speak of expertise in your subject or in bribing?

"Time is one of God's most precious gifts to us. Corruption wastes time. Your professor has already wasted two years of your life. Just calculate our national loss because of this culture of corruption.

"Corruption harms the poor the most. How does he force his male students to bribe him? Can they get their doctorates if they can't bribe or serve him?

"Corruption kills our conscience and brutalizes our character. Why do you think our police have reached a point where they can commit cold-blooded murder of innocent citizens simply because they are Muslims, Sikhs, or Christians? Corruption has already blinded your professor to the feelings of his own wife. Does he care what adultery would to do to your family and children?

"Corruption enslaves us – what does India's 'freedom' mean if you are not free to live an honest, righteous life?"

"Corruption is, of course, evil," responded Manju hesitatingly and slowly, "but what if two consenting adults wanted to sleep with each other? That wouldn't be corruption would it?"

"Would it then be wrong if your husband killed you because he was jealous?"

"What do you mean?" asked a startled Manju.

David opened the Bible to chapter 20 of the book of Exodus and began explaining the Ten Commandments to Manju. "Corruption is evil because God says 'You shall not covet your neighbour's wife or property.' Murder is sin because God says, 'You shall not commit murder.' Adultery is sin, because God says, 'You shall not commit adultery.' When we break God's law we sin. Sin enslaves and destroys us.

"Our lives are miserable because we are sinners. Your husband does not love you anymore and that is sad. But should you therefore seek love from another man? Your husband is a sinner because he is violating God's word, 'Husbands love your wives.'[25] If you commit adultery, you too would violate God's law. Do two wrongs make one right? What your husband needs is the Saviour who would save him from his sin.

"But my question is, what's wrong with adultery? Why should God forbid what everybody does or at least wants to do?" Manju asked.

"Everybody covets something that belongs to someone else.

That is why we need God's law. God commands sexual purity because sex outside of marriage destroys its main purpose."

"And what is that purpose?" Manju wondered.

"The first two chapters of the Bible tell us that in the beginning God created the heavens and the earth . . . and the Spirit of God was moving over the waters on the earth . . . and God said, 'Let there be light and there was light'. So this universe was created by God, His Spirit and His Word, who eventually was incarnated as His Son, Jesus. This triune God – Father, Son and Spirit – said, 'Let us make man in our image', so He made humans in His image, male and female, to be 'one.'

"Each of us is God's image, but when we give ourselves to love another person we become more like God. Sexual love especially makes two people 'one flesh.'[26] When the two become three by having a child, they become more like God, because that is when they understand more of the parent-like heart of God – they care for their weak children, as He cares for us. The human family, thus, is meant to reflect the image of the triune God. God the Father, God the Son, and God the Holy Spirit have been one through all eternity. God desires a similar permanent oneness for us, especially in our family life. The primary purpose of human sexuality, therefore, is to cement human family, to make us one and keep us one. That is why lack of love in a family, whether the parents divorce or children rebel, hurts so much. Adultery or unfaithfulness in marriage is evil because it violates our oneness, the image of the triune God in us.

"You are drawn to sin because your heart is as sinful as your professor's, though you may have less opportunity to sin than he does.

"The question is: Should you reinforce your professor's corruption or help him find a spiritual transformation that would make him a genuine servant to his students, as he is supposed to be and as he is paid to be?"

Chapter Three

A Temple in the River*

Four young men cycled 30 miles in late September 1977 to visit me. They had heard that my wife and I, having studied in the West, had come to serve the poor in their district.

"The flood has washed away our homes, cattle and crops," they lamented. "Can you please come to our village, see for yourself, and do something?"

I agreed, without realizing that even getting to their village would be a challenge. The flood had washed away the mud road. The last four miles had to be trudged. On arrival I found their colony deserted.

"They have gone to cremate a dead body," an old woman informed me.

I was anxious to return home before dark as I had left my wife and infant daughter on our farm, in the middle of nowhere, in this *dacoit*-infested district. The *dacoits* are armed gangs of (generally) upper caste robbers who loot, kidnap and kill at will, dodging the police for decades.

---

* Although the events of this chapter are true, some of the discourses are recreated from recollections of my discussions with those young men during that visit and over the subsequent months, interspersed with further reflections.

The cremation ground was also deserted. They were now in the river, bathing. The beauty of the river stunned me; no one had ever told me that our district had such scenic spots.

The young men were not expecting me. They seemed surprised that I had kept my word. With great delight they showed me the pride of their village – a magnificent stone temple in the middle of the river. "This temple is 1000 years old," they boasted, "built around the same time as the Khajuraho temples."

The Khajuraho temples I knew. Planeloads of tourists came daily to see the erotic sculptures. I was surprised that I had never heard that historic monuments like these were also hidden away in our district. What moved me more, however, was the contrast between this stone temple and the villagers' mud dwellings.

"Why do you think," I asked them, "you are so poor?"

Oh!" One of them thought aloud, "We work hard for 10 years, save money, buy oxen, build houses, and then these floods come. Everything is lost. We have to start all over again. This has continued for countless generations; so we are poor."

"One thousand years ago," I provoked him to think, "Our forefathers built this magnificent temple in the middle of the river. Obviously they had great engineering skills, organizational powers, surplus wealth and time. This temple has withstood a thousand years of floods. Do you think back then they had the ability to build houses on the banks of this river that could withstand floods?"

"Of course, they did!"

"Why then didn't they build safe houses as well?"

"They did build some flood-proof homes," said one of the young men, pointing to the village chief's large stone house, sitting on the highest point of the village.

"Exactly!" I agreed, "It was not the ability they lacked but the permission to build proper housing. But let's talk about that in a minute; first tell me something else: Do you think that the priests and rulers who built this temple had the ability to build dams and canals?"

"Certainly!"

"You're right again! In some parts of India, dams were indeed built. Why do you think that ability to build dams was not utilized in any significant way in our history? If they had, today we would be richer than Switzerland. In this climate we could have been harvesting four crops a year if this water had been tapped."

The young men looked puzzled. The question had never been raised.

"Was this temple built to worship the river?" I gave them a clue.

"Yes, the river is our mother. She gives us life. But she can also take life when angry."

"That's the problem. Our ancestors feared, deified and worshipped the river. That's why they built temples, instead of dams. People that fear and worship nature become incapable of governing nature. Their belief-system prevented our forefathers from saying to the river, 'We love you, so we'll build a home for you. Please don't go away in summer, stay right here. During the monsoon, we will make a canal, so you can go into the jungle, instead of flooding our homes.' It was left for the British to come here and start building dams to maximize our ability to make full use of the rivers that God has given us.

"Why did our fathers worship rivers instead of regulating them? One reason was that they believed that the river was greater than them. It existed before they were born and would continue long after they were gone. The British started building dams because they believed that human beings were greater than nature because they were made in God's image. God gave each of us abilities of wisdom, understanding and knowledge like himself.[1] God, our heavenly Father and Creator, wanted us to rule over this earth – not appease her with worship and sacrifices. Our fathers did not know what the river was, who we were, what our relationship with nature ought to be, because they did not know God."

"They were very religious," countered one of the young men.

"They certainly were, but I'm not talking about religion. I'm talking about truth. Is the river a goddess? Are you born a Shudra because of your bad karma? We must seek and find truth, not believe superstitions and lies. False beliefs are far more destructive than floods. They make us internalize slavery. You do need immediate relief from the after-effects of the flood. But in the long run it is truth that will liberate you."

Over smoky cups of tea, made in a lid-less saucepan over firewood, the young men and I continued a lively discussion on the question of truth.

The temple and the chief's house were made of stone. The rest of the upper castes lived in relatively better mud houses in safer parts of the village. The untouchables were forced to live in mud huts in lower, vulnerable parts of the village. The physical structure of the village reflected the social hierarchy of the community.

No one disputed that Hinduism had forced vulnerability, poverty and squalor upon the nation. For my new friends life had indeed been suffering; but should that suffering be accepted or challenged? Should they learn to meditate on their "inner bliss" or find relief – start irrigation systems, be bold enough to build stone houses, and discover truth that would liberate them – from the lies that were at the root of their misery?

My friends already knew that their "untouchability" and poverty were related. So our discussion centered on my thesis that an important factor behind their suffering was that they had been enslaved by false gods – sinful human beings, nature and evil spirits. They worshipped Brahmins who told them that they were "untouchables"; they worshipped demons that demanded all kinds of sacrifices, sometimes even their children; and, for a thousand years, they had tried to appease the river instead of managing her. In order to be liberated from their misery they needed to be liberated from these "deities."

I shared with them the story of the Israelites who were slaves in Egypt. God sent Moses to deliver them from their slavery. After they came out of Egypt, God gave them Ten Commandments so that they might preserve their freedom. God said to them: "I am the Lord your God, who brought you out of Egypt, out of the land of slavery. You shall have no other gods before (besides) me. You shall not make for yourself an idol in the form of anything in the heaven above or on the earth beneath or in the waters below. You shall not bow down to them or worship them."[2]

False gods enslave but the true God liberates, I explained. God told the Israelites that the first requirement to preserve their liberty was to stop worshipping false gods. These should not be worshipped, because, *first of all*, they are not gods. There is only one Creator God. All other beings are created by him.[3]

Take for example the Brahmins. I have many good friends who are Brahmins. However, just as I have sinned, so have my Brahmin friends. The Bible says God is holy, and that "...all have sinned and fall short of the glory of God..."[4] God's Holy

Spirit convicts each of us equally when we sin against God and one another.[5] Brahmins, like all of us, need God's grace and forgiveness. No one is closer to God by virtue of his birth in a particular family. All of us need to return to God with repentance and faith.

God is love.[6] Brahmins must be loved because God loves them, just as he equally loves all other sinners.[7] Brahmins must be respected because they equally bear God's image along with every other person.[8] However, to call them "maharaj" and to touch their feet as though they were gods is to believe an enslaving lie.[9] India will be liberated from many of its miseries when it acknowledges that Brahmins are not gods but sinners.

Similarly, I continued, neither are finite spirits divine. Only God is the Creator. All other beings are created by him. Some of the spirits are demons, awaiting God's judgment at the end of this age. Some call them "*devtas*"[10] but they know very well that they are only "*levtas*."[11] Those spirits keep demanding and extracting. In the Gospel of Matthew we read how Jesus freed two men who had been possessed and oppressed by evil spirits. When they first saw Jesus, the demons shouted, "What do you want with us, Son of God? Have you come here to torture us before the appointed time?"[12] Not only did Jesus free those oppressed by demons, he gave his disciples the authority to drive out demons:

> He [Jesus] called his twelve disciples and gave them authority to drive out evil spirits and to heal every disease and sickness.[13]

After his death and resurrection, just before he ascended into heaven, the Lord Jesus commissioned his disciples (including all who follow him now), saying

> "All authority in heaven and on earth has been
> given to me. Therefore go and make disciples of
> all nations . . ."[14]

I assured these incredulous young men that I
personally knew this to be true because I had seen people
delivered from demons in the name of the Lord Jesus.[15]
For thousands of years our people have lived in fear and
slavery of demons, worshipping them as gods and
goddesses. The Lord Jesus not only frees us from their
slavery, he gives each of his disciples authority to cast out
these demons.

Secondly, I continued, we should not worship rivers, trees,
animals and forces of nature because God created
human beings to rule over the earth, not to worship it.
After God created our first parents Adam and Eve, he said
to them,

> "Be fruitful and increase in number; fill the earth
> and subdue it. Rule over the fish of the sea and
> the birds of the air and every living creature that
> moves on the ground."[16]

Some Europeans and Americans are now coming to
India to teach that we should not rule over nature, but
"flow with nature." But they themselves did not flow to us on
the ocean waves. They flew over the oceans. They could fly
over the airwaves because their parents had learned to rule over
nature. If you choose to flow with nature, it will flow through
your houses — like the last flood.

We must respect nature because we don't own it.

God owns everything and everyone.[17] He made each of us equally his stewards. We must love nature as our Father's handiwork. We must manage and tend it to make it a beautiful garden as he originally intended.[18] The Bible warns that God holds each equally responsible. He will destroy those who destroy the earth.[19] He gave us the right to rule over the earth, not to destroy it, but to manage it. However, to worship creation instead of the Creator is to replace the truth with an enslaving falsehood.

I told my attentive audience that *thirdly* we are told not to make images or idols of God or to bow before them. The moment we allow a priest to make our god we automatically give him the right to dictate our socio-religious norms. Priests are also sinners; therefore, they will naturally invent moral systems that suit them. They will tell us that we must touch the feet of their sons, pay astrologers to make all our decisions,[20] and celebrate special days and occasions with appropriate fees for them. Man-made religiosity is exploitative, if not vulgar. We only have to see the erotic sculptures in Khajuraho: they embody a spirituality designed to sexually exploit women.[21]

Fourth, the living God wants a living relationship with us, his children, I explained. We hang photographs of our loved ones in prominent places in the house and garland them respectfully only after they are dead. But God is not dead. To a Samaritan ("untouchable") woman who had been taught that God had to be worshipped on a sacred mountain, Jesus said,

> "God is Spirit, and his worshipers must
> worship in spirit and in truth."[22]

Worshipping created beings or things: an angel, an idol, a human being, a mountain, a river, or an animal is not worshipping as God desires. To substitute a creature for the Creator is not the truth.

Fifth, we are told not to make images of God because God has already made his own image – the human being – both male and female.[23] If we want to love and serve God's image, we need to love and serve our neighbours. The practice of untouchability is one of the most powerful arguments in favor of the commandment against idolatry. The priests who teach us to worship rivers and mountains, snakes and demons, also teach us to treat some human beings as "untouchables." The true God, our Father, on the other hand commands us to love all his other children equally as we would love ourselves.[24] Each person belongs equally to God.[25] He wants us to teach and train each child about God and his ways.[26]

Although we are God's image, we have sinned. This means that God's image in human beings has been marred. Human sinfulness, however, cannot be an excuse for hating human beings. Would an idol-worshipper despise an idol simply because its nose or one of its arms is broken? Obviously not! You don't despise God's image simply because it is damaged. God himself wants to restore his image in us. That is why he sent the Lord Jesus, his sinless incarnation, into the world. The Lord Jesus is the perfect image of the invisible God. Restoration of God's image in us means allowing God's Holy Spirit to transform us to become increasingly like Jesus.

It was time for me to start my return journey. But my friends were so fascinated by what they were hearing that they decided to walk back the four miles to the paved road with me. They wanted to continue the conversation.

One of them asked me a pointed question:

"Are you saying that the Hindu religion is false?"

I asked a counter-question: "Are human beings equal or unequal?"

"Our religion says that we are unequal," replied one of the young men, "but our Constitution says that we are equal. How do we know which one is true?"

Modern India's Constitution is anti-Hindu because it is based on the biblical ideas of justice and human equality. God is just, he is our Lawgiver, and he is the Judge of the entire world.[27] He has given each person equally a sense of justice and fairness. God gives each person equally a right to justice. This principle of an equal right to justice was the foundation of the Magna Carta (1215). By the security of Magna Carta, every person is given the right to petition for and obtain redress of a grievance of any breach of that charter even by the King, his Chief Justice, or any official. The Magna Carta said:

> If we (the king), our Chief Justice, our officials, or any of our servants offend in any respect against any man, or transgress any of the articles of the peace or of this security, and the offence is made known to four of the said twenty-five barons, they shall come to us - or in our absence from the kingdom to the Chief Justice - to declare it and claim immediate redress.[28]

This biblical principle of equal justice in the Magna Carta is consequently the foundation of the British, American and Indian Constitutions. (This is very different from the Law of Manu, which treats Brahmins differently from Shudras before the law and on property ownership). Thus each Dalit and Brahmin has the equal right to legal protection and justice under India's Constitution because of God's character as revealed in the Bible.

God holds every judge, leader and legislator especially accountable as they represent him to people. That is why in modern democracies judges, leaders and legislators take an Oath of Office in the name of God ("so help me God") to uphold "impartial justice" and to "to preserve, protect, and defend the Constitution."[29] People uphold justice when they learn about God, and act in the "fear of God" knowing they will each have to account to him for every word and deed.[30]

The fundamental constitutional principle of equality was explicitly expressed politically in the American Declaration of Independence, which begins with the preamble, "We hold these Truths to be self-evident, that all Men are created Equal, that they are endowed by their Creator with certain unalienable Rights, that among these are Life, Liberty and the Pursuit of Happiness ..."

God has equally made each person unique. He has equally gifted each of us with special abilities and prepared good works for each of us to do.[31] The fathers of America's Independence were right in affirming human equality, but they were wrong in believing that human equality was "self-evident" to those who did not know God. We see every individual to be uniquely gifted by God with different physical, mental, emotional, financial or social aptitude and capital. While God gives each of us differnt resources and abilities to be stewards of, he holds each of us equally responsible for how we manage them.[32]

By not understanding how God made each person equally like him, yet equally unique and equally responsible, the "Aryan" Nazis in Germany believed inequality to be a "scientific" or a demonstrable truth. Equality was self-evident to the founders of American Independence because they had come to know God through the Bible and by the principles of "Natural Law" as shown in God's creation.[33] Human equality is based on God's character as revealed in the Bible.

The truth is taught in the very first chapter of the Bible, which says that God created man in His image: male and female.[34] Both men and women were created equally in God's image. This is very different from the Vedic idea that the Creator made Brahmins from his head, Kshatriyas from his arms, Vaishyas from his belly, and Shudras from his feet,[35] or Manu's teaching that women are inferior creatures on par with animals.

The third chapter of the Bible gives another reason that makes human beings equal. It says that Eve, the first female, became the mother of "all the living."[36] God created each male and each female person equally with the ability to marry and bear children – regardless of ethnic background, "race" or "colour." We are brothers and sisters because we are all God's image and also because we are all descended from the same parents.

The chapter gives a further reason that makes us equal. It tells us the story of how all human beings sinned, though they had been created good. Much of the Bible contains the sad story of human degeneration. So the fact that all human beings are sinners also makes us equal. Sin separates us from a holy God. It means that Brahmins are as far away from God as any Shudra. No one is holy or close to God by being born in a special family. Every human being equally needs to come to God individually to find forgiveness for one's sin and freedom from the power of sin.

Although the Bible vividly portrays the ugliness of human sin, its message is the "Gospel," literally "good news." It tells us that God is love and that he loves the whole world. Jesus said,

"For God so loved the world that he gave his one and only Son that whosoever believes in him shall not perish but have eternal life."[37]

We are equal because we are equally the objects of God's love. We are of equal worth in His sight. We are each so precious to God that He gave His only Son to become a sacrifice for our sin. The world may call some "Shudras," but for God your value is equal to the value of the blood of His beloved Son that was shed on the cross of mount Calvary. Brahmins may say you are born into a particular "caste" and that makes you unequal. But God's gift of forgiveness to you by the blood of the Lord Jesus Christ makes you equal to all other human beings.

The Gospel has another exciting implication for transforming India: It says that God is our Saviour. We are equal because God offers every one of us the opportunity to become a child of God's love through repentance and faith in Jesus Christ. By virtue of being made in God's image we are already God's children. But because of our sin and rebellion against God we are children of God's wrath. When he judges us at the end of this age, he will punish our rebellion in hell. The good news according to the Bible is, Jesus

came to that which was his own [the Jews], but his own did not receive him. Yet to all who received him, to those who believed in his name, he gave the right to become children of God – children born not of natural descent, nor of human decision or a husband's will, but born of God.[38]

That means every sinner can equally become a child

of God's love by receiving the Lord Jesus as his or her Saviour and Lord. A woman does not have to be re-born as a male to find salvation, nor does a Shudra have to be reborn as a Brahmin to find God. Salvation is not by natural birth or reincarnation but by a spiritual rebirth. As Jesus explained to an enquiring Jewish rabbi, Nicodemus,

> "I tell you the truth, no one can enter the kingdom of God unless he is born again."
>
> "How can a man be born when he is old?" Nicodemus asked. "Surely he cannot enter a second time into his mother's womb to be born!"
>
> Jesus answered, "I tell you the truth, no one can enter the kingdom of God unless he is born of water and the Spirit. Flesh gives birth to flesh, but the Spirit gives birth to spirit."[39]

God equally gives those who believe on the Lord Jesus the gift of his Holy Spirit to live within.[40] He equally adopts them into his family. He equally appoints each to be a king to rule under Jesus the King of Kings.[41] He equally appoints each to be a royal priest with full access to worship in his temple and to minister to other people.[42] God gives each believer his royal "robes of righteousness" and a mansion in heaven.[43]

The signers of America's Declaration of Independence took human equality to be a self-evident truth because that is the revelation of God's character and the consequence of the Gospel on which they had been nurtured. Human beings are equal because anyone can become God's beloved child by faith in Jesus Christ.

"That sounds good in theory," a young man challenged me, "but don't many Christians also practice inequality and caste?"

"They certainly do," I admitted. "Some of those great Americans who declared their faith in human equality themselves owned slaves. American democracy did not give voting rights to women until 1920. Christians are sinners like all other human beings. The point is that if you commit yourself to truth it begins to transform you. American society was forced to resolve the contradiction between what it believed and what it practiced. Truth transformed America. Slavery had to be abolished; equality of male and female had to be given legal expression. That could not have happened if America, like Nazi Germany, had believed in the superiority of the Aryan or Caucasian (white) races, or of the male over the female.

"Not only the Christians in America, even Christ's own disciples did not practice equality. They had seen Jesus publicly reject untouchability, when he asked the Samaritan woman for water,[44] ate with tax-collectors,[45] touched the leper,[46] healed the servant of a Roman Centurion,[47] allowed a prostitute to wash his feet with her tears of repentance and gratitude,[48] and allowed a woman with an hemorrhage to touch him and get healed.[49] All the above people were "untouchables" according to the religious Jewish leaders of that time.

"The disciples received Christ's command to go into the entire world and make disciples of all nations.[50] Yet, when the crunch came, even his closest disciples like Peter[51] could not overcome their racial prejudice, break traditional barriers and eat with non-Jewish 'gentiles.' Untouchability continued in the Jewish section of the early Church. The Apostle Paul and others had to fight against it, because it was a violation of God's truth.[52] Eventually the truth liberated the Church; the first Church Council in Jerusalem formally repudiated untouchability.[53] It was this resolution to abolish untouchability, which made

Christianity an independent religion,[54] rather than a sect of Judaism. The Jews continued to treat non-Jews as untouchable 'gentiles.'"

God confirmed this truth of equality for all he saves by revealing to his disciple John that in heaven there is "a great multitude that no one could count, from every nation, tribe, people and language, standing before the throne and before the Lamb.[55] God guarantees to take people from every background to be with him in heaven, not just Brahmin men.

* * *

The young men did not want me to leave. But goodbyes had to be said. Some months later, five of the young men decided to become followers of Jesus Christ and were baptized. Within a year they had managed to get an electric line into their village, obtained a bank loan, installed an electric pump, and built a little water tank to irrigate their fields.

However, a few years later, after we had moved out of that district, I learnt that upper caste men in connivance with some petty officials had forged official documents and snatched the lands that my friends had brought under irrigation. The truth had begun to transform them but India continues in her slavery to her traditional "religiosity" and consequent injustice. God is just and compassionate. He is particularly concerned that the poor and oppressed, aliens, widows and orphans are treated justly and kindly. God holds each person equally accountable and will reward and punish each for their actions.

Chapter Four

The Leper*

Sandhya and Sooraj were both Brahmins. They lived barely a mile apart in Manohar Nagar, but they met only after Sandhya joined the same college. Their love at first sight upset Sooraj's classmate Kiran. She had never revealed her secret crush on him. In contrast to herself, Sandhya appeared flamboyant.

Kiran played it dirty. She called Sandhya's home and without identifying herself told them about her love affair. Sandhya's grandmother became agitated. She forced Sandhya's father to investigate the matter immediately, "to save family honour."

The father went to the college looking for Sandhya. Kiran had told him that Sandhya might have gone to a movie with her boyfriend. Sandhya returned home that evening to face her trial before a troubled family.

She pleaded that there was some misunderstanding as she was at college the whole day. She may have gone to the ladies' room when her father had visited. No one believed her.

"We are paying for you to study, not to fool around," was

---

* Although inspired by the gruesome murder of the Australian missionary Graham Staines and his two sons, this treatment for a filmscript is a work of fiction. It is written in response to Indian Prime Minister Atal Behari Vajpayee's call for a national debate on conversion.

her father's verdict. The grandmother declared that she had always been opposed to the idea of girls going to college. Because, if Sandhya was not already pregnant, it was only a matter of time before she would be. "Who will marry her then? In any case, she has already brought dishonour to the family. The whole town must be talking about them."

Sandhya's mother tried to prevent her from being beaten, but she was pushed aside. Sandhya was locked up "in her own best interest," besides that of "protecting the family's honour." She was not allowed to go to college or to use the phone "until you've learnt your lesson." The idea was floated to send her off to an aunt's home "to keep her away from this boy."

Sooraj telephoned Sandhya, only to get abusive threats from her grandmother. That evening his 13-year-old brother Gaurav came to him to get help with his maths homework. Sooraj was unusually kind; he not only helped him but also gave him money to buy a kite... if only Gaurav would deliver a letter to Sandhya.

Gaurav liked the challenge of an adventure. The next day he was at Sandhya's home, pretending to be her "girlfriend's brother." He had come to collect his "sister's poetry"! Sandhya's unsuspecting mother let him in. He passed on the letter and was invited to "come back with new poems."

Gaurav and Sandhya become fond of each other. Gaurav was thrilled with her kisses on his cheek and money for movies from his brother.

Just as Sandhya's family began cooling down, her father ran into a college student with his scooter, fell, and hurt himself. Blaming him for hitting their friend, some students started beating him up. In what seemed like a coincidence from a Bollywood[1] film script, Sooraj helped rescue and take him to a nearby clinic.

The family rushed to the clinic. First the father and then Sandhya introduced Sooraj to the family! The episode restored their relationship and culminated in marriage.

The wedding was a joyous affair. The next day the newlyweds went to the temple to offer *pooja.*[2] As they come out, the first person they saw was an aggressive beggar with leprosy. Sandhya was irritated. "Why do you have to be the first to show your face to us?" She complained to the priest who tried to drive the beggar away. But Sooraj intervened, arguing for compassion. "We must give alms to the needy," he said, "as though we are giving to God."

The marriage was blessed by the birth of two children. Sandhya's father was transferred to another state. So Sooraj's extended family, including the family of an uncle – his father's elder brother – became her only family in town.

On and off Sandhya began to complain to Sooraj about numbness in her fingers: they seem to be losing sensitivity to heat and pain. Sooraj, however, was too busy with his work to pay attention to such "minor matters." Until one night, while undressing her, he saw what seemed like leprosy patches! Their worst fears were soon confirmed. Sooraj would no longer touch his wife, nor was Sandhya allowed to embrace her children. Her mother-in-law blamed her disease on her "bad karma."

Once again, Sandhya was locked up – this time in a dark, dingy servant's room behind the house – until the family could decide what to do with her. Gaurav argued that she should be taken to a doctor; his father agreed. The uncle, however, argued that this would make her disease public, making it difficult for their children and grandchildren to marry into good homes.

Unable to agree on what to do, the family kept her in that room, hidden from the world. Sooraj pined for her, but didn't know what to do. He started drinking. Sandhya pined for her children, but was not allowed to see them. Gaurav managed to bring them to her on those rare occasions when the grandparents took their afternoon siesta, the cousins had gone to school, the three men were at work, and the two ladies had gone shopping – all at the same time. Otherwise Sandhya consoled herself with gazing for hours at the children's photographs, pasted on the wall.

The inevitable happened: Sooraj began an affair with another woman at work. One day he brought her home to get to know his family and children. Through the cracks in her door, Sandhya saw the woman trying to befriend her children who were playing in the backyard. Much to Sooraj's and his family's embarrassment, Sandhya became loudly abusive. The new woman was upset at not having been informed about Sandhya, his "mentally disturbed wife." She dashed off in a rage.

Later that night, the elders agreed that the subject could not be postponed anymore. The grandfather explained that to solve this kind of problem, the ancient tradition was to burn or bury the lepers alive. "A violent end delivers them of their bad karma and ensures a healthy reincarnation," he pronounced. "The natural death of a leper, in contrast, results in four births, followed by a fifth as a leper! It is those ignorant British who banned our ancient tradition. What is the use of the miserable existence of a leper anyway?"

Gaurav was horrified that his family could even entertain the idea of killing a human being…his brother's wife…sweet Sandhya. "That is a crime and a violation of her human rights!"

The uncle countered, arguing that even enlightened opinion in the western world now favoured "assisted euthanasia." Ancient Indian wisdom was in perfect harmony with modern science. Species and races evolve only as the "unfit" lose out in the struggle for existence. It's survival of the fittest! The interest of the family must override individual rights. The children needed a mother and Gaurav would not find a wife if the community got to know of her disease. He needed to think of his brother and the children, not just of his favorite sister-in-law. His concern for Sandhya had blinded him to his brother's needs, even though it was Sooraj who was now supporting Gaurav's university education.

Gaurav was furious. "I thought my family was better than those that torture and kill their daughters-in-law for a larger dowry," he protested. The father was unable to take such a strong accusation. "This situation could not be compared with dowry-death," he countered. "They are inspired by greed. Euthanasia is 'mercy killing,' done in the interest of a patient whose life has become a burden to herself."

A phone-call for Gaurav interrupted the family conference. Gaurav hung up the phone and informed the family that his friend needed help to prepare for an examination. They would be up most of the night, so he would return home only the next day.

After midnight, once everyone was asleep, Gaurav took Sandhya out of her room and drove her on his friend's scooter to the leprosy mission asylum outside the city. He had already explained the situation to the missionary doctor. They had agreed to keep Sandhya hidden to guard her family's honour.

Early the next morning, sleeping over at his friend's, Gaurav was awakened by a call from his frantic father. Sandhya was missing! The family had searched for her but could not find her. They assumed that she had either committed suicide or run away to some holy city to become a beggar. He should come home right away. Gaurav refused, accusing them of murdering her secretly while he was away. After a sobbing Sooraj pleaded with him, Gaurav agreed to return home.

The missionary family kept Sandhya in their own home and not in the asylum. She couldn't believe that they would treat her wounds with their own hands. As their children began playing with Sandhya, it seemed a whole new life had begun for her.

Neelu, a tribal girl, who was also a part of the doctor's family life, befriended Sandhya. Neelu was preparing herself to start a school in her tribal village; she especially wanted to teach the Bible to her people and was therefore studying it with the doctor's wife.

Neelu and Sandhya ate with the missionary family. One evening the younger son asked his father, "Dad, will there be McDonald's in heaven?"

"Why do you ask?"

"Cause I am sick of eating rice everyday. I like Big Macs. Jesus said that if we sacrifice something for him we will receive it tenfold in heaven."

"Don't talk nonsense," the father was irritated, "I take enough nonsense during the day running this institution; do you have to add to it in the evening?"

"I'm sorry sweetheart," the mother intervened. "My food may not be as interesting as McDonald's, but if you help me, tomorrow we can sure try making something that you like. In fact, we should go for a picnic where Dad and you can play. He needs a break from all his work."

"We've got to be grateful that we have electricity and a refrigerator," the daughter added. "Remember when Dad first came here? There was no running water, no electricity, no fridge and no road. He had to live in a mud hut."

The older brother joined in: "Yes, and how much did Jesus sacrifice when he came to save us?"

The mother tried to lighten things up, "If McDonald's can make a Big Mac surely you could make a small one. That is, if you learn to cook. Some of us here only like eating, not helping in the kitchen."

One day Sandhya asked, "Doctor Sahib, why is your family able to love me – a leper – when my own family wanted to get rid of me?"

"If you had a fever or a cancer, would you become a 'fever' or a 'cancer'?" the doctor asked?

"What do you mean?"

"I mean you are not a 'leper.' You are a human being just like any of us. You just happen to have a disease called leprosy. We have to treat you as we would treat any other patient."

"I never thought of that! But you aren't treating me as a patient, you have made me a part of your family, when my own family rejected me!"

All three of the doctor's children wanted to answer simultaneously. So each was permitted to give a short answer.

The youngest explained that they touch and serve leprosy patients because Jesus touched and healed them.

The older boy answered that God loves the whole world. He wants everyone to have abundant life. That's why he sent Jesus to give life.

Instead of replying, the daughter asked a question: "Why did your family want to kill you?"

Sandhya explained the theory of karma and also the social problems: her husband needed a wife, the children needed a mother. If the caste found out about her disease, her brother-in-law and cousins would not be able to get married either. Her own children would be ostracized because of her.

The doctor's wife explained that we are all guilty of bad karma – sins – but we don't have to suffer for them, since Jesus has taken all our sins upon himself on the cross.

Neelu, the tribal woman, put forward her point of view: She had given up belief in karma, since everyone used the theory to justify the misery and exploitation of the tribal women.

"Did the drunkards abuse their wives because of their wives' karma, or because of their own sinfulness?" The fact is that after these husbands repented of their sin and asked Jesus to save them, the liquor shop in their village had become the adult literacy centre. Like her, the other women had also been freed from their karma. They were learning new skills. She herself would soon become the first woman teacher in the history of her tribe!

Sandhya told them that the theory of karma was not the only governing principle in their family. The more educated also talked about "the survival of the fittest" in the struggle for existence. They said that even the West was now justifying "mercy killing."

The doctor joined the table talk saying that they served the sick, oppressed, and downtrodden because the Bible had shaped their thinking. The Bible says that we cannot love God unless we love our neighbours. Just as a mother pays more attention to a child who has a special need, God wants us to take special care of the sick, the weak, the "unfit." As sinners we are all unfit, we don't come up to God's standards of righteousness, we can't enter his holy presence. But Jesus, the sinless one, gave his own life to make the unfit, fit: fit for the kingdom of God. He forgives repentant sinners. Our sin makes us fit cases for punishment. But by taking our sin and its punishment upon himself on the cross Jesus has made forgiveness possible. He makes us fit to become God's beloved children.

"But. . ." Sandhya's sentence was interrupted by the doorbell. The pastor walked in with an evangelist and Neelu's uncle whose hand and head were in bandages. There had been trouble in Neelu's village and her brother and uncle had been beaten.

At the time of sowing the landlord had not paid full wages to Neelu's family; in retaliation the labourers refused to harvest the landlord's fields. Since several of these labourers had become Christians, their new audacity was blamed on their faith.

The former liquor contractor joined hands with the landlord; together they approached the local MLA[3] to prevent Christianity's spread further in their area. They brought a fascist group to the village that believed that Christianity was a foreign religion.

"Christianity is destroying our culture: the wives no longer respect their husbands, the labourers do not respect the landlord, the converts no longer go to the temples or pay the priests, the astrologer has stopped coming to the village because very few use his services. Christians speak against our gods; they say these idols are not god; converts don't observe our sacred traditions, so the priests are now migrating to the cities. Christians are asking us to believe a foreign god and follow alien scriptures and traditions. People who are not loyal to our culture cannot be expected to be loyal to our country. If the spread of Christianity is not stopped, the Westerners will once again become our colonial masters."

The doctor took the visitors to the home of the District Magistrate.

Sandhya began studying the Bible with Neelu, who invited her to the Church on her last Sunday there. Neelu was to be "dedicated" by the church elders for the mission of starting a school in her village. Sandhya was reluctant, as she was not allowed to appear in public.

Guarav had kept visiting Sandhya. One day as they walked around a little pond, he told her that her husband, who thought she was dead, was planning to remarry. Sandhya was shocked. She asked if he could bring her children to visit her. Gaurav said that her children also believed that she was dead. This was better for them. In any case, he could not risk her being discovered.

Sandhya, in tears, accused him of not being a good and resourceful enough friend. Gaurav was upset. He was not cowardly, he protested, just prudent. He had done the best he could. His family might have kicked him out had they discovered what he had already done for her. He was still dependent on them to complete his studies. In any case, she had to take the consequences of her karma.

Sandhya retorted that the talk about karma was nonsense. She preferred the idea that Jesus Christ had taken her sins upon himself. She now believed in resurrection, not in reincarnation. After his death Jesus was resurrected from the dead. His tomb was empty. He did not reincarnate in another body but his own body had become glorified. This gave her hope for her own degenerating body. It affirmed her individuality. She would always remain herself, not become another person.

Gaurav was horrified: "Have you become a Christian?" He reminded her that she had already brought sufficient shame upon the family. Conversion would be the last straw – absolutely intolerable. He tried to persuade her against conversion, by arguing that there is only one God, religions are different roads to reach the same goal: "So, what is the need to convert?"

"Of course, there is only one God," agreed Sandhya, "But suppose there is only one diamond in this pond..." She stepped into the pond and picked up a stone before continuing... "would you pick up any stone and say that it was the diamond? If there is only one God then we must seek him, not pick up any snake or scorpion and believe that it is God."

Gaurav had forgotten that his sister-in-law was a college graduate. He said, "I hate missionaries because they convert the poor, the illiterate, the tribals, the sick. Why don't they try to convert *me*?"

Sandhya retorted, "Jesus said, it is the sick that need a doctor, not the healthy. Your family, so conscious of its superiority and honour cannot confess its spiritual need. I'm a victim of your family's notion of its spiritual superiority. I'm grateful that the missionaries you hate did not leave me at the mercy of your family's inhumanity. Yet, I'm not bitter because I know that I am as sinful as anyone else. But why should you be upset if I ask the Lord Jesus Christ to save me from my sin...And as far as the illiterate tribals are concerned, I am grateful that Jesus sent these missionaries to deliver Neelu's family from the tyranny of the village priest, landlord, liquor contractor, and the politician that would keep them in bondage forever."

"But why should you convert to a *foreign* religion?"

"Because truth has nothing to do with national divisions. Everyone must accept what is true, no matter where it comes from. If a cure for leprosy is found in one nation, should not all nations accept it? Physical leprosy is a much smaller problem compared to the leprosy of our hearts. The day after my marriage I saw a leper outside the temple and cursed him. I didn't realize then that I already had spiritual leprosy in my heart. By treating that leprosy patient as an "untouchable," I insulted the image of God in him.

"My conversion does imply rejecting some beliefs and values that I inherited from my culture, but what I'm accepting is truth, not something foreign. It is the truth about the sickness of our soul, about finding healing for our inner leprosy. You and I will have to give accounts of our lives to God. When we treat others as untouchables we sin because we disobey God's command to love our neighbour as ourselves. Our sins make this world a hell, but eventually they will take us to a real hell. Therefore we need to repent of our sin and get reconciled to God and to our fellow human beings. This spiritual transformation is true conversion."

Gaurav couldn't understand how Jesus could die for the sin of the world. Sandhya explained that it was no mysterious philosophy: everyone who saw Jesus hanging on the cross saw clearly that it was not the justice of the world that was hanging on the cross, but its injustice, cruelty and evil. Jesus was innocent; he became sin because the world was sinful. But as he prayed on the cross, "Father forgive them for they know not what they do," his death became a sacrifice for our sin. Jesus became the sacrificial "Lamb of God" that takes away the sin of the world, making reconciliation and peace possible.

Gaurav ridiculed the idea that a person could take on someone else's karma. Sandhya tried to explain her new faith, as best she could. But their conversation broke down on the point that each one must bear one's own karma. "It is cowardice" concluded Gaurav, "for me to commit a crime and ask someone else to take my punishment. I must take the punishment for what I have done. Each person must work for his own salvation."

Neelu finished her course and the special church

service of her dedication to God's service was around the corner. Sandhya wanted to begin her social life again. So she agreed to go to the church with the Doctor's family.

That Sunday evening Mr. Samuel Paul, the hospital administrator, came to visit the doctor's family with a box of sweets. Sandhya was sitting with the doctor's family at the dining table.

"This box of sweets," he said, "is to celebrate the new property we have been given in Calcutta by my in-laws."

Mr. Paul asked Sandhya who she was. She gave him evasive answers about her parents but said nothing about her in-laws. Mr. Paul was perceptive enough to realize that she was hiding her true identity. That made him curious. He went to Neelu, who was getting ready to go to her village, gave her some sweets for her family, and found out more about Sandhya.

Later that night the pastor came to see the Doctor Sahib. He reported the rumour that Mr. Paul's new property was not a gift from his in-laws but a result of the money he had been making at the institution's expense.

"How can that be!" asked the doctor.

"The community believes Mr. Paul takes kickbacks from the suppliers of medicines, but the bulk of the money comes from the contractor who is building the new blanket-weaving center for the asylum."

"That's rubbish," retorted the doctor, "We took quotations from three different builders."

"Brother," the pastor seemed exasperated, "people are beginning to lose their respect for you. They say you hold them accountable for trivial matters and demand perfection, but you are blind to the crookedness of the really wicked."

"But where is the evidence for wickedness?"

The pastor produced documents to show that two of

the construction firms were just "letterheads." The same contractor, a friend of Mr. Paul, had given all three quotations.

Doctor Sahib confronted Mr. Paul the next morning. The hospital administrator was livid and vowed to destroy the institution if he was disciplined. The hospital committee suspended his services pending full investigation. To take his revenge, Mr. Paul informed Sandhya's family that she was alive, in the neighbourhood, with missionaries, and had been converted. The family was furious. They decided that the missionary doctor must die for converting their daughter-in-law.

Sooraj's uncle contacted the local wing of the fascist organization that had been speaking against missionaries as "a threat to the nation." The fascists agreed to help the family. They asked Mr. Paul about the missionary's movements and found out that the doctor was going to Neelu's village to inaugurate a new school. He would also be preaching in the annual camp that the mission held in that village. A conspiracy was hatched: The liquor contractor and the landlord offered to provide the manpower, and the MLA offered the political cover.

The missionary and his two boys were getting ready to go to Neelu's village in their station wagon when the District Magistrate called the doctor and counseled him against going to the village where Christians had been beaten already. "There might be trouble," he said ominously. The doctor felt that the best way to defuse the tension was to talk to the landlord. The pastor who had come to say good-bye also suggested that the doctor should take the DM's advice seriously.

The doctor, however, was determined to go: he needed to encourage and teach the new believers; the plan to open the school had been announced long ago; people would be coming from many villages to the annual camp. Besides, Jesus had said that when the good shepherd sees the wolves coming he does not leave the sheep in search of his own security. He lays down his own life to save the sheep.

The school dedication ceremony had to be postponed as the village chief (the landlord) announced that he needed to go away, unexpectedly, to visit a sick relative. The camp, however, began as announced. During the day the doctor examined patients, and the boys assisted their father. In the evening the doctor preached sermons on God's love while the boys operated the slide projector.

On the third night, tired from the day's work, the boys fell asleep during their "Family Prayer," because their father was going on and on praying for the village chief. He prayed that God would heal his sick relative so that the chief may return to the village before the end of the camp, so that the doctor may be able to talk to him, so that harmony may be restored between the chief and the church, and on and on. . . When no one said "Amen" the doctor realized that his prayer partners had already gone to sleep. Gently, he covered them with a sheet and kissed them "good-night" on their foreheads. Within moments of lying down he too was fast asleep.

The mob that appeared suddenly out of the shadows of the tree was not all that quiet. Yet, the noise they made did not wake up the doctor. What disturbed his sleep was the suffocating heat. It took him a few moments to realize that he was about to be roasted alive in his car. He grabbed his sons in both hands and kicked open the door. But three sets of tridents pushed him back with mob chants of *"Jai Hanuman."* He attempted to go to the driver's door, but it was too late. The gas tank exploded like a bomb. The doctor collapsed as his sons cried in terror and, hugging them, he prayed: "Lord use this fire to turn us into torches that would light up this nation."

The gruesome murders made international headlines. Sandhya's family was watching the funeral on TV. Some of them began feeling guilty when they heard the doctor's widow forgiving the murderers. His daughter thanked God that her father was "found worthy of dying for Jesus." Suddenly, the camera focused on Sandhya comforting the widow and her daughter.

"That's Ma!" exclaimed Sandhya's son. "She's not dead. She's alive. She's holding the doctor's daughter!"

The TV crew caught Sandhya saying to the widow, "I understand your pain. My husband is alive, yet I am a widow. I am here, yet my children are orphans."

Sooraj stood up crying. "Yes, your mother is alive and well. We are sick. Her doctor died because our conscience is dead. Let's go get Ma."

"Wait! Think! Don't act emotionally!" said his uncle with trepidation.

"I've thought for weeks," said Sooraj. "I've talked for hours with your friends who killed him. I've debated with Gaurav. It is not *thought* that I have lacked, but courage. India is not going to be saved by eliminating the doctor, but by emulating him. He was the true nationalist, who loved India and Indians. I'm as proud of my rich heritage as anyone else, but there is much in our hearts and in our culture that needs changing. It is not force that we need to save our culture, but the freedom to change the evil within us."

Gaurav met Sandhya as she was returning from the funeral. She asked him if he still believed that the religion of the fascists who killed Doctor Sahib was the same as the religion that gave her a new life.

"Doctor Sahib was practicing and preaching God's love in daylight," she said. "The children of darkness struck under the cover of night. Whoever converts them out of their darkness is the best servant of India. Now I understand the meaning of the cross. I should have been the one to die because of my disease, and because of my family's inhumanity. The doctor lived and died to save me . . . like Jesus did."

They were still talking when Sooraj arrived with their children and embraced Sandhya, with tears rolling down his face.

Chapter Five

Where Should Satish Go?

by **Shri Om Prakash Valmiki** ©

December's freezing days prevented the weak sunlight from easing the cold, and an icy wind pierced through clothing and flesh, chilling the bones.

Mrs. Pant had finished her little chores around the house, and sat wrapped in a blanket knitting a sweater for her daughter. Loneliness intensified the cold; it was almost time for her daughter to return. Sonu would demand food as soon as she barged in the door. Anticipating this, her mother had already prepared a meal for her and kept it in the kitchen.

Mrs. Pant was startled from her reverie by loud knocks on the door. They became persistent as she wondered who it could be. In the quiet house the banging sounded like it would tear the door off its hinges. Sonu never knocks this way. . .Sonu's father doesn't. . .Neither does the tenant, Satish. . .And besides, Sonu's father doesn't get home till six; Satish gets home at four or four-thirty. . .Who could it be? Mrs. Pant wondered as she hesitantly opened the door.

Two strangers, a man and a woman stood outside: old, withered, muddied, and exhausted. The woman's gaunt face had suffered the ravages of time; the wasted appearance of the man seemed to suggest some chronic disease.

"What do you want?" Mrs. Pant barked.

The old couple was startled, and flinched from her angry eyes, as if they had been caught red-handed in a crime.

Their silence only aggravated her all the more. "Who are you? What do you want?!"

The man cleared his throat and began, "Namaste ji. . ." He held up his hands in greeting.

"What's the matter? Why were you banging my door down like hooligans?"

The old man made another fumbling attempt to speak, then gestured to the house and blurted out, "Is there a boy named Satish living here?"

Mrs. Pant was taken aback: Why were they looking for Satish? "Yes...he lives here. Why do you want to know?" she probed.

"You see. . .Madam. . .he. . .we. . ." The man stuttered, then grew silent. The woman beside him spoke. "Madam, we haven't seen him for six months. Can you please call him and tell him we're here?" Her eyes began to glisten with tears.

"No, he's not here. He's at school. He won't be back till the evening. But who are you?" Watching their haggard appearances and their uncouth ways, Mrs. Pant was growing leery.

The man made another attempt to speak. "Madam. . . he. . ." The woman nudged him with her elbow. "Madam," she said, "What can we say? We've suffered so much. . . Our miserable fates. . . And he's been here the whole time. . . We've looked for him for six months. Let him come back. We'll wait here till he comes." She wiped her damp eyes with the corner of her dirty sari.

"You can't wait here at my doorstep looking like

beggars! Tell me – who are you? Why've you been looking for him?" Mrs. Pant's curiosity could not be appeased.

Hesitating again, the man said in a pleading voice, "I'm his father. This is his mother." Each word came out painfully.

Mrs. Pant gasped, as if the sky had cracked open. Satish . . .their son! How was it possible? She couldn't believe it. "Why did he leave home? Was there an argument?"

The woman wiped her eyes again. "I don't know Madam, I don't know what he was thinking. We asked him, 'What's the point of studying more? Get a job, start a business, then you can get married. . .' but without saying anything, he just left home. We searched and searched. . . finally to discover that he's now living here."

A memory flashed through Mrs. Pant's mind: Sonu, tying a *rakhi*[1] on Satish's wrist, adopting him as her brother. Satish trying to hide a sudden tear in his eye. That day he had ceased to be just a paying guest who was renting a room in their house, he became a member of their family. He had captured not only Sonu's heart, but also the hearts of everyone in the household.

The woman's words shook Mrs. Pant's faith in Satish. She had imagined him to be from a good family. "He's not here right now. When he comes, I'll let him know. Where do you live?"

"We live in this town, in Indresh Nagar, near Kavali Road."

"In this town?" Mrs. Pant's incredulity was transparent.

"Yes, Madam," the woman replied.

"All right. . .Please leave now. . . I'll send him as soon as he comes home." Mrs. Pant was anxious that they leave. It was important that she shouldn't be seen talking to these people by Mrs. Gupta, her neighbour. If Mrs. Gupta saw her, she would no doubt have a thousand prying questions. She would want to dig up all the information: "Who are these people? What do they want?" God forbid Mrs. Gupta should find out that these are Satish's parents! Mrs. Pant could just imagine the gloating in her neighbour's voice if Mrs. Gupta found out that Sonu had tied a rakhi on Satish and adopted him as a brother!

"Please leave. . . I'll send him." Mrs. Pant was eager to shut the door.

"Madam, we won't cause any trouble. We haven't come here to make trouble. It's been six months since our child has been missing from home. We searched everywhere! Finally, we heard something from Balsar who sweeps your street. He lives in our neighbourhood in Indresh Nagar. Balsar the sweeper told us that Satish has been living here." The boy's mother tried to gain the landlady's sympathy. "Madam, you are a woman, you know a mother's pain. Let us wait here till he comes. We'll take him with us when we go."

Satish, a Bhangi,[2] from the sweeper caste, living in my home! Satish the Sweeper! Mrs. Pant was livid.

She heard Sonu's footsteps and her calling: "Mummy, quick, give me some food; I'm starving!" Sonu hesitated when she saw two strangers at her doorstep, then ran inside. Without another word to Satish's parents, Mrs. Pant rushed into the house behind her daughter, leaving the door half-open.

Satish's clothes were drying on the clothesline in the courtyard. Mrs. Pant brushed past them as she entered the house. It sent a shudder up her spine ... as if something filthy had touched her. She stormed into the house, grabbed a broom, and used it to knock Satish's trousers and shirt off the clothesline. She fiercely swept them away into a corner of the courtyard, like pieces of offensive garbage. She was shaking in anger.

The afternoon turned into evening. Satish had not

returned. The old couple spent four hours in silence outside the house, enduring them as if each hour was a year. They didn't speak a word to each other. Both stared at the ground, or gazed into the street. They lapsed back and forth between reality and memories of their son.

Mrs. Pant's full attention was upon her front door. Mrs. Gupta could arrive any second, and she would create a scene in the street. Mrs. Pant was at a loss for what to do. At the same time, she was furious with Ravi Sharma. He was the one who had brought Satish to their home — didn't he know what Satish's caste was? If he knew, why hadn't he told them? Why had he deceived them like this?

Sonu was almost finished with her homework, when there was the sound of a scooter in the street. "Mummy, Papa's home!"

Sudarshan Pant parked his scooter in the courtyard and called to his wife, "Who are those people sitting at our doorstep?"

"Satish's parents," Mrs. Pant called out in reply.

"They look quite poor! Are they low-caste? Where's Satish?"

"He still hasn't returned."

"How long have they been sitting outside?"

"Since the afternoon."

"Sitting like that since the afternoon, on the street? You could have brought them in to sit in the courtyard, at least!"

"Yes. . .that's all that's left to do now, isn't it?" came her sarcastic reply. "As if it wasn't enough to invite a sweeper to live in our house. And how many times Sonu has eaten from his plate! I don't know what to do, how will we ever cleanse ourselves of this pollution? And what if Mrs. Gupta hears about this — we'll never hear the end of it, and the whole town will find out! 'Mrs. Pant kept a sweeper in her house as a tenant! If I had known, I wouldn't have let him set foot in my house!' That's what she'll say to everyone. As soon as he comes, grab his things and throw them out on the street. Even his clothes have a foul stench. . ." Mrs. Pant's normally rosy cheeks were flushed with rage.

Sudarshan Pant stepped outside the house. "Where have you come from?" he asked.

"From Indresh Nagar, near Kavali Road." Satish's father's eyes were moist now.

"All right — you leave now. As soon as Satish comes I'll send him to you." Sudarshan Pant was curt. He turned to go back into the house, then stopped and said, "Look, you don't need to come here again. Only respectable people live here."

The woman's eyes filled with tears again. "Sir, we will be very grateful. Our son left home angry. Please explain to him that he should come back. . .Tell him we're worried."

With faltering steps the couple began to walk back toward their side of town. They turned back and gazed at the house repeatedly, as if Satish might suddenly appear. Their frail old bodies soon faded into the darkness of dusk.

Satish returned home late that night. He had gone straight from school to the factory. Ijaz Sahib, the factory owner was a kind and just man. The first time Satish came to him, requesting a job, Ijaz Sahib had patted him on the back and said "Be brave. You will reach where you want to go in life. Just work hard and keep pursuing your education."

For the last six months Satish had been going to school in the mornings and then would work in Ijaz Sahib's light bulb factory until nine or ten at night. He earned about Rs.20 a day, and from this came his money for the fees at

school, for his food, and for his rent to the Pants. His room
at the Pants' was more of a closet — just enough room for a
string cot. All he had to his name were his schoolbag and books,
two sets of clothes, a straw mat, a cotton sheet, and a blanket.
Even the blanket was a new acquisition, as he had only recently
been able to afford it.

Today he had gone straight to the factory from school.
There was a lot of work to do at the factory, and when he
returned home he found that the front door was locked.
He heard the sound of pots and pans from the kitchen.
Satish knocked lightly on the door.

"Is that the boy?" Mrs. Pant shouted immediately from
within to her husband. "Tell him to pick up his things and leave
right now!"

Sudarshan Pant tried to placate her. "Where will he go?
It's late at night. He's a child. . .Let him leave in the morning.
He has been like a brother to our daughter, are you going to
throw him out of our house like this?"

"How else should I tell him to go? Should we bid him a
fond farewell? He dared to pretend that he could be my
daughter's brother — enough is enough! I refuse to let him
live in my house another minute!" Mrs. Pant's shrill voice
carried through clearly to Satish.

On the doorstep, Satish's ears were smarting, as if live
coals had been held to them.

"Tomorrow morning I'll call Ravi Sharma and bring
him here. We can discuss this in front of both of them."
Sudarshan Pant tried to hold back his wife's anger for the night.

"I have nothing to discuss with Ravi Sharma! What makes
you think I'm going to let him into my house either — who
knows, maybe he isn't even a Sharma! For all we know
he's a *Chamar!*⁸ Give these low-caste people an inch, and they'll
take a mile!"

"But Satish isn't like that; you know he's never taken advantage of us. Have you ever seen him behave disrespectfully? In the morning when Sonu asks where Satish is, what will you say to her? She's just gone to sleep, and you know how many times she asked for Satish before she went to bed. Do you have any idea what she'll go through when she finds out that we kicked him out?"

"I don't know. I don't care. Tell him I want him to leave right now. He deceived us all these months, he deserves it." Mrs. Pant's decision was final.

In spite of the bitter cold outside, Satish had broken into a sweat. Part of him wanted to scream, and to break down the front door with an enraged kick. He stepped back as he got ready to kick, then stopped, took a deep breath, turned abruptly and left the house, his blood boiling within.

As he left the Pant's lane and reached the main road, Satish decided to head for the bulb factory. The road was deserted in the cold. A few yellowed lamps illuminated the boy's path, but a deep blackness settled itself over his soul. Hungry, thirsty, and tired from a full day at school and then at work; all he had had to eat was a parantha that Mrs. Pant had given him that morning. He usually cooked for himself in his little room, but today he had been in a hurry and couldn't prepare anything. Then, after school, he had gone straight to the factory on an empty stomach, only drinking a cup of tea he had bought from a nearby tea-shop. After work Ijaz Sahib had given him fifty rupees, which were still in his pocket. He needed to buy a textbook: that would cost thirty-five rupees. His thoughts were jumbled and confused. He pulled his scarf and wound it tighter around his head, covering his ears.

Sudarshan Pant's home was about six kilometers away

from the factory. At ten o'clock on this winter night there was very little likelihood that Satish would be able to find an auto-rickshaw to take him to the factory – and it would probably cost fifteen or twenty rupees. He decided to keep walking. The bridge over the river was cloaked in darkness. The Mall Road was shrouded in the night, and so was Chakrata Road.

Satish's feet were numb, but he tried to keep a quick pace. If he were lucky, maybe he would find Ijaz Sahib still at the factory, because he usually worked till midnight.

There was silence as Satish reached the factory-yard. The broken tin gate of the factory was swung half-open as usual. The ground was sprinkled with shards of glass and wire filaments from broken bulbs. Picking his way through these, he reached the factory, and stepped in.

It was warm inside and a welcome relief for Satish. He saw the yellow light bulb of Ijaz Sahib's office, which meant that the boss was still there.

In those cave-like rooms of the factory, cobwebs hung from cheap tin roofs and scrap materials lay scattered on the floor. Ahmed and Santha were still at work near the furnace. In the light of the fire from the furnace, Ahmed looked more like a shadow than a man. His health had been deteriorating for the last three months, and his bones were becoming prominent. Satish saw pain in Ahmed's eyes. No worker lasted more than two to three months at this factory, either because of the nature of the work or because of illness.

Ijaz Sahib was a good man, but unconcerned about the upkeep of the factory; his own "office" was no better than any of the tin-roofed storerooms.

He was startled to see Satish come in, with his schoolbag hung over his shoulder, exactly the way it had been when he came in to work in the afternoon.

"You haven't gone home yet?"

Satish stood without speaking. He was at a loss for what to say, or how to begin.

"Sahib. . ." he began, but the words got stuck.

"Yes, what's the matter? You look upset." Ijaz Sahib looked at the boy's face closely. In the dim yellow light Satish looked helpless and tired.

"Sahib. . . can I stay here tonight please?" Satish asked softly. To Ijaz Sahib it seemed that Satish was standing far away, in darkness, and he thought he heard a tremor in the boy's voice.

"What? You want to spend the night here? Aren't you going to go home?"

"I have no home, sir. I left my father's house because he wanted to get me a sweeper's job with the municipality. He was going to retire, and was frantic to have me take his place. He ran around trying to negotiate for me to get this position, and had talked to his boss. It was a matter of two thousand rupees. My father had made an arrangement to pay all this — two thousand rupees so that I can spend the rest of my life with a sweeper's broom in my hand! They want me to forget about studying, sir, and take this job, but I don't want to be a sweeper — I want to be educated. I feel like I'm suffocating in that neighbourhood — not because the people are poor or low-caste, but because of the quality of their lives. They are so accepting of their lot in life, of their fate! They've never seen that life can be different, that their world can be different.

"Ravi Sharma is my math teacher. He was the one who arranged for me to live with the Pants. Their family became like my own; they gave me so much. They have a little daughter, who is in the seventh standard. When she's dressed in her school uniform in the morning she looks like a little angel – she tied a rakhi on me and adopted me as an older brother. But today. . .today they found out, now they know my caste. Sir, does being a Bhangi mean that your relationships have to be broken? I want to be liberated from this Bhangi identity, sir. I didn't deceive anyone. They never asked me about it, so why would I tell them?

"My exams for school are very near. I need a place to stay. Sir, was I born just to be a sweeper? I want to do so much more with my life than just clean streets till I die." His voice broke with suppressed sorrow.

Ijaz Sahib was listening intently, watching Satish's glistening eyes.

"Look, I know you're a hard-working boy. You're responsible. You work and I pay you. You don't take favours from me, and I don't take favours from you. Beyond that we have no relationship – you work, I pay you. If Mrs. Pant has kicked you out of the house or you left your parents' house I really can't help you. I'm a businessman, and we have a business relationship. This is your personal problem; you handle it. This isn't an ashram[4] where any needy person can come along and expect charity. There's no place to live in this factory, look somewhere else. You have my sympathy, but I can't help you." Ijaz Sahib flatly refused.

Satish's hopes were shattered like a broken bulb. He had walked this distance with a glimmer of hope inside, but now that too had faded into the night. He had not prepared himself for the rejection or the hollowness of Ijaz Sahib's "sympathy". On every side he felt darkness closing in on him.

With defeated steps he turned to leave, walking away from Ijaz Sahib, the furnace, and the shadow that was Ahmed. The night was deep and dark outside. Satish walked with slow steps, in an uncertain direction. The silence was broken only by the sharp whistle of a night-watchman from a distant neighbourhood. The whistle seemed to cry out, "Where should Satish go?"

———————

© **Om Prakash Valmiki.**

Note – Shri Om Prakash Valmiki (born 1950) works for the Ministry of Defense. His poems and novels have been published by various Hindi publishers and publications. He has acted in and directed several plays. The story "Where Should Satish Go?" was first published in Hindi by *Lokmat Samachar* in 1993. The English translation is by Ms. Anandit Mangalwadi.

For reflections on this story please see the next chapter, "Conversion As Revolution."

Chapter Six

Conversion as Revolution

Dr. Ambedkar and Conversion

In 1916, Baba Saheb Dr. Bhimaro Ambedkar became the first "untouchable" to receive a Ph.D. in Economics from Columbia University, New York. He returned to serve Maharaja Gaekwad in Baroda who had sponsored his studies. Even as a minister of the princely state, Dr. Ambedkar could not find a room to rent. His caste folk had no spare rooms; those who did, would not rent it to him.

He was the chief in his ministry. Yet, his subordinates would not touch him. The clerks had to bring papers to him for his signature, but instead of giving them to him in his hands they would throw them on his table. Needless to say, he was not "allowed" to go to their tables.

Dr. Ambedkar endured the humiliation. But working in Baroda became impossible after the upper castes managed to get him evicted from the only hotel room that a Parsi proprietor had rented to him. He left for Bombay (now Mumbai) and became a professor of Economics at the Sydenham College of Commerce. Two years later he went to England to study law. He earned a Doctor of Science degree at London University, returning to the Bombay High Court in 1924. His merit and fame did not give him dignity. The upper castes became so jealous and irritated by this that they made life extremely difficult for him and ultimately hounded him into the public arena.

Baba Saheb began his public life by leading a campaign to enable his community to use the public well in a suburb of Bombay, where he was then living. On Christmas day of 1927, he created a stir by publicly burning a copy of *Manusmruti* - the code of Manu – the most important religious document that the Brahmins use to justify the caste system and untouchability. The same year he was appointed a member of the Legislative Council of the Bombay Presidency.[1] His campaign to enable "untouchables" to worship in a Hindu temple in Nasik made him a national figure. In 1930, the Prime Minister of England invited him to represent the depressed classes in the famous Round Table Conference, where serious discussions regarding India's independence began. By 1933, Mahatma Gandhi had begun to see Dr. Ambedkar as his chief rival for leadership of the lower castes.

Mahatma Gandhi went on his longest "fast unto death" to deny the depressed classes the right to elect their own legislators. To save Mahatma Gandhi's life, Baba Saheb surrendered that most significant political tool that the British Prime Minister had given to the lower castes. Yet, the upper castes kept heaping insults and abuses on him. Thus from 1916-35, for two whole decades, Dr. Ambedkar tried to find liberty and dignity for himself and his people through education, employment, political power and socio-legal activism. His experiences led to deeper and greater frustration. So finally, in 1935 he made his revolutionary announcement: "I was born a Hindu, I had no choice. I will not die a Hindu because I do have a choice."[2]

This was not an impulsive decision. Baba Saheb had thought about the subject of conversion deeply enough to write a whole book on the matter, *Annihilation of Caste*. His thesis in that book was straightforward: the Hindus do not ill-treat the lower castes by reason that Hindus are worse than other human beings. In fact they are as good or as bad as any other people on earth. The Hindus practice caste and untouchablity because it is a part of their religion. Therefore, the only way to annihilate caste is to cease being Hindu.[3]

In spite of having thought through the matter in the 1930s, Baba Saheb waited for a decade, for India's independence. He was given the honour to serve as the Chairman of the Constituent Assembly, to help shape free India's Constitution. He gave us a Constitution that abolished untouchability and affirmed every human being's intrinsic dignity. Yet, in his mature years his conviction continued to grow that it was not the Constitution, but conversion alone that would liberate his people from the bondage of caste. So, in 1956, a full two decades after his resolution to not die a Hindu and shortly before his death, Dr. Ambedkar led over 300,000 of his followers out of the Hindu fold into Buddhism.

What would Dr. Ambedkar say to a person like Satish? No one who knows anything about Baba Saheb will dispute that his advice to Satish, as well as to the high-caste Mr. & Mrs. Pant, would be that to become human they have to quit Hinduism. Hinduism did not dehumanize Satish alone. It had so enslaved the Pants that they were not free to do what was right either. Hinduism prevents its adherents from loving fellow Hindus and thereby, it weakens India.[*]

Conversion And The Birth Of Modern India

Dr. Ambedkar's thesis, that conversion was the best available

---

[*] The references in this paragraph are to the story in Chapter Five "Where Should Satish Go?"

means of India's emancipation, was not original. Modern India was born in the battle to secure every individual's right to convert. Charles Grant was one of the two "fathers" of modern India.[4] He was the first person, in 1786-87, to advocate the view that "light was the true cure for darkness."[5] Secular and Hindu historians have tended to downplay, if not condemn, Grant's pivotal role in Indian history precisely because he advocated education for conversion as the only civilized means of India's regeneration.

Many people dismiss the idea of conversion without understanding the subject. They may say, "Oh! All religions are the same; so what's the point of conversion?"

Well, because all ice creams are "the same," would you kill someone because he prefers mango ice cream instead of chocolate?

Obviously not!

So, why in recent years have fascist Hindus gone to the extent of burning missionaries alive? Is it because they are mindless murderers?

Far from it! Brilliant men lead the Sangh Parivar; they understand what Dr. Ambedkar knew: conversion is revolution. It challenges the *status quo* and changes lives and history.

East and West had been interacting for over two centuries before Grant sent his long proposal for India's regeneration to John Wesley.[6] India's experience with European traders, soldiers and rulers had been disastrous. The peasants of Bengal had lived under oppressive despots from time immemorial but the East India Company's rule made their life much more miserable.

Up until Grant's own spiritual conversion, East and West had interacted only in terms of profit and power, trade and war. Grant grasped that India's regeneration required that it interact with ideas, principles and values that had created the modern

West. A clash of armies might crush India, but a clash of worldviews would bless. Writing in an era of illiteracy and superstitions, *sati* and human-sacrifice, demon worship and temple prostitution, Grant argued that it would be irresponsible for the Western Church to leave India to her fate or in the hands of European soldiers. The Company's misrule required correction; missionaries were also needed[7] to educate, enlighten, and regenerate India – especially her morals.

Unfortunately, because John Wesley was preoccupied with other commitments, he was not able to assume responsibility for India. So Grant sent copies of his proposal to 14 church-leaders and Christian politicians, including William Wilberforce. Only Rev. Charles Simeon, Fellow of King's College, responded to Grant's plea. He began preparing some of the best students in Cambridge, like Henry Martyn and Claudius Buchanan, to give their lives to serve India. After 1790, Grant became a friend of William Wilberforce – the outspoken evangelical Member of Parliament. That connection helped Grant become the Chairman of the East India Company and a Member of Parliament. He used these positions to begin India's renaissance.

Grant was attracted to Wilberforce because the latter was leading a national campaign against slave trade. Sadly, even some Christian gentlemen in England were engaged in the slave trade, just as some Indian Christians continue to practice casteism. Wilberforce's position was that Christianity and slavery were antithetical. So Grant assumed that Wilberforce would support his mission for India's emancipation from her multi-faceted slavery.

Grant sat in the boardrooms while Wilberforce was the public mouthpiece. Together, for over twenty years, they lobbied the British Parliament to permit missionary enterprise in India. Many Members of Parliament were share-holders and directors of the East India Company. They opposed missions, evangelism, and conversion for two reasons. *First*, the Company directors did not want to be exposed as greedy, heartless merchants. Evangelicals like Wilberforce were already exposing the brutality of British Companies in Africa. The MPs knew that conflict of interests were inevitable between Englishmen who went to India to make money through means fair or foul, and missionaries who would go to serve the natives.

The *second* and more important reason was that the MPs knew that their military conquests had made the ruling classes in India hostile towards them. Missionary criticism of Hinduism and Islam would threaten the religious leadership of India. And the Company would not withstand the combined opposition of both the political and religious leadership of India. These fears were not unfounded. The Hindu leadership was as intolerant of criticism as was the Muslim. Sure enough, the missionaries[8] soon began opposing evils like untouchability and sati. But the British were so afraid of meddling with India's social system that it took a quarter of a century (from 1803-1829) for the Company to muster up enough courage to ban an obvious social evil like *sati*.[9]

Eventually Wilberforce and Grant succeeded in building up the pressure of public opinion on enough MPs to make missionary enterprise legal in 1813. Their argument was that the state should not use coercion for social change. Genuine change has to come from within. Therefore, while a person should have freedom to believe that untouchabilty is "purity," his opponents should not be prevented from saying that untouchability was "impurity" and "inhumanity." It would be immoral for the British Parliament to value the economic interest of a British Company so highly as to deny religious freedom — the source of social transformation

– to her subjects. The state must give freedom to its subjects equally to practice their beliefs as well as to question them.

Reforms often begin when a minority begins to question cherished ideas of the dominant majority. Such questioning results in debates, a quest for truth, conversion and social transformation. Conversion, at the very least, involves rejection of falsehood, repentance for sin (which earlier generations may have considered righteousness) and acceptance of higher moral norms. A society that curtails criticism of dominant cultural ideas and takes away citizens' rights to change their beliefs and practices becomes closed and authoritarian. It becomes weak by reducing to mindless obedience its citizens who then become slaves, not willing participants.

Grant did more for India than win the battle for her spiritual liberty. Here it is sufficient to say that it was Grant's battle for missions and conversion that gave birth to a liberal and tolerant India. Without Grant, there would not have been a Ram Mohun Roy, Jotiba Phule, Gandhi or Ambedkar. All reformers and missionaries would have been eliminated, as effectively as the killings of Mahatma Gandhi and Graham Staines.

Conversion As Revolution

Dr. Ambedkar was not alone in his belief that without the unbridled right to conversion, the Constitution would remain an ineffective piece of paper. Conversion's power is well understood by its opponents. Recently a journalist went to a court in Orissa where Dara Singh is being tried for allegedly burning alive the Australian missionary, Graham Staines, and his two sons in January 1999. One of Dara Singh's supporters told the reporter that he was sorry for Staines' boys since they were innocent, but he did not feel sorry for the burning of Graham Staines, because he had been converting people. Another supporter of Dara Singh, a lawyer, rebuked the accomplice. "Don't be so sentimental," he said, "Staines was coaching his sons to follow in his footsteps; just imagine how many Hindus those boys would have converted had they been allowed to live?" How could anyone justify burning little boys alive? Such are the "justifications" made by those who know the power of conversion to change the *status quo*.

"But must a Graham Staines attract others to his faith through acts of charity? Doesn't service lose its nobility when undertaken with a motive to convert?"

Did not the Lord Jesus heal all who came to him and command his followers to do likewise? Yet it is true that some Christians run social service projects primarily for personal aggrandizement. Some may use their acts of charity as bribes to lure others into their faith. Yet, in spite of such shameful abuses by some petty Christians, the fact remains that genuine Christian service is hated because it is a greater threat to the Hindu social order than the phony ones. Consider this scenario:

Kallu grazes his landlord's cattle. He is an illiterate, landless, poor, "untouchable" peasant who dresses in rags and goes barefoot. He gets a little cut on his dirty feet, which turns septic. He goes to the village doctor who sells him an ointment. The ointment is good, but ineffective without proper washing, bandaging and shoes. Kallu has little sense of hygiene and the upper caste doctor isn't going to wash a Shudra's feet. The infection ulcerates and spreads. Kallu is not able to keep his job, his family is not able to pay for his treatment, so he is thrown out on the streets of Calcutta to beg and die. His family loves him, but is unable to cope with a white elephant whose "karma" is taking him to an early death. His caste may be sad for him, but the rest don't care.

A Mother Teresa (or a Graham Staines) comes along and interrupts Kallu's "karmic" suffering. The missionary is scandalized that a family and a culture can discard a human being with such indignity. She washes the "untouchable"'s feet with her own hands. She not merely treat him but also appeal to generous Western donors to help feed him.

The missionary believes that she is simply obeying Jesus' command to love her neighbour as herself. She does not have the faintest idea that in fact she is stirring up a revolution. She has thrown down a gauntlet at a three housand year old worldview and religious system. Kallu is shocked to discover that he is not an "untouchable," that he is in fact precious.

Why?

The missionary says that she loves him because God does and because he commanded us to love our neighbour.[10]

"How do you know God loves me?"

"I know because He sent his Son to take your sin upon himself. Jesus shed his blood as the sacrificial lamb of God to save you from eternal death in hell."

Kallu cannot believe that anyone loves him, let alone that someone would love him enough to die for him. But the missionary is irrefutable evidence that someone does love him and holds him precious. Kallu is attracted to the missionary's belief system. His family is overjoyed by the new life that has been given to him freely. They want to convert to the new faith; in fact, their whole caste has become interested in exploring a worldview that affirms their dignity.

The upper castes in their village are infuriated that their slaves want to escape their slavery. Weren't these folk born to serve us because of their bad "karma"? Do they now want to become our equals? Will these missionaries educate these sub-humans and make them officers – our doctors, inspectors and judges? Who will then graze our cattle? If upper caste landlords don't prevent Kallu's conversion, their economy, life-style and culture would indeed be ruined.

What are the options open to the upper castes?

To prevent conversions out of Hinduism they could attempt:
   (a) To outdo the missionary's service. But what if their religious system does not give them inner spiritual resources, nor even permit them to touch, let alone serve the downtrodden, and thus meet the challenge of the missionary's service? In that case their second option is
   (b) To condemn her, and forcefully prevent her from serving the likes of Kallu. But if they can't get the government to throw the missionary out of the country then, they claim their only option is
   (c) To murder her.

Spiritual conversion and social service cannot be separated. To be real, inner transformation must reform our external culture, which, in spite of all its beauty, has much that is corrupt and oppressive. God says you cannot love Him unless you love his image – your neighbour. If God loves the unlovable sinners – us – then how can we claim to be God's children without loving the unlovely and the unlovable – the "lepers" and those discarded and marginalized by our society?

The Lord Jesus said that it is not the healthy but the sick that need a physician. "The Son of Man came to seek and to save that which is lost."[11]

Should the healthy be allowed to prevent a doctor from treating the sick? Should the servants of the poor be intimidated by the politically powerful who demand that missionaries ought to run schools and colleges for children of the elite, but not go out to serve the downtrodden tribals?

The Conversion Debate

Fascist Hindus began persecuting Christians especially in the tribal areas of Gujarat in 1998. Atal Behari Vajpayee, the Prime Minister of India, went on an official visit to try and prevent bloodshed. Toward the end of his visit he called for a "national debate on conversion." A section of the press and many Christians accused him of transferring the blame that belonged to his comrades – the perpetuators of violence – to the preachers of peace. I, however, do not think that Atalji was only using diversionary tactics. He sensed what was soon confirmed by the brutal murder of Graham Staines: that a revolution – an explosive social revolution – is indeed brewing in India.

Millions of Mauryas* and Satishes have now arrived at the point that Dr. Ambedkar had reached in 1935. They have realized that education, employment, constitutional rights, and political power are insufficient to liberate them from the indignity of caste. If they want liberty and dignity for their children then they have to throw off the yoke of a two-millennia old oppressive religious social order. This revolution would go much deeper than throwing off the British Raj. It would involve examining and changing our beliefs, values, traditions, practices and culture. The beneficiaries of the caste system, who have a vested interest in preserving the status quo, would naturally resist this revolution. The murder of Graham Staines and hundreds of incidents of persecution that preceded and followed that incident demonstrate that a section of the politically powerful Hindutva movement is determined to use force to preserve its position of privilege, and if possible, to coerce or forcibly "reconvert" people to their previous slavery.

Technically, Graham Staines himself was not converting anyone. His murderers, however, held him morally responsible for

*See Chapter One: "What Enrages Dr.Maurya?"

the conversions that took place in the area. The murder, therefore, raises two basic issues over which national consensus needs to be achieved:

(1) Force or Freedom – Will India become a great nation when forced to accept a Hindu cultural unity, or will it become a great nation by the freedom to critically examine our traditional beliefs, customs, and cultural values and where necessary to change ourselves?

(2) Healing: Physical or Spiritual also – Must we honour a Mother Teresa or Graham Staines only if they heal our physical leprosy, or do missionaries deserve honour for also offering healing for our social and spiritual sickness?

Force Or Freedom

India has legitimate reasons to be proud of its democratic freedom. Very few societies have been able to sustain liberty for very long. Much of the world around us, especially in Asia, Africa, and the Middle East, continues to live under the oppression of force and dictatorship. Nor did European Christendom permit liberty during much of her history. Why is the option of force so seductive given the fact that the practical advantages of freedom are so obvious?

It is individual liberty that makes a nation great by making it possible for each person to be creative. At the beginning of the second millennium, that is, around the year 1000 AD, Chinese civilization was hundreds of years ahead of the West in technology. The Arab nations were at least three centuries ahead of the West. Within Europe, around 1500 AD when the Portuguese conquered Goa, Spain and Portugal were a century ahead of Northern Europe. The Dutch and British international trading companies did not even begin until around 1600. Why did nations, which are now called "underdeveloped," not maintain their techno-economic lead? Why did they lose out to nations like England, Holland, Germany, Switzerland, and later North America?

Macro-historian David Landes points out in his landmark study, *The Wealth and Poverty of Nations: Why Some Are So Rich And Some So Poor,* that a common factor behind the stagnation of every single one of these nations was their decision to close their mind to the challenge of alien religious ideas. The nations that opened their minds to new ideas, beliefs and values surged ahead.

> When the Portuguese conquered the South Atlantic," writes Landes, "they were in the van[guard] of navigational technique. A readiness to learn from foreign savants, many of them Jewish, had brought knowledge that translated directly into application; and when, in 1492, the Spanish decided to compel their Jews to profess Christianity or leave, many found refuge in Portugal, then more relaxed in its anti-Jewish sentiments. But in 1497...Spain led the Portuguese crown to abandon tolerance...From then on, the intellectual and scientific life of Portugal descended into an abyss of bigotry, fanaticism, and purity of blood...Abraham Zacut and other astronomers found life in Portugal dangerous enough to leave in droves. They took with them money, commercial know-how, connections, knowledge, and – even more serious – those immeasurable qualities of curiosity and dissent that are leaven of thought.
>
> That was a loss, but in matters of intolerance, the persecutor's greatest loss is self-inflicted...As in Spain, the Portuguese did their best to close themselves off from foreign and heretical influences. Education was controlled...the life of science and speculation decayed . . . the bulk of the people were disinclined to

independence of thought and, in all but a few instances, too much averse from intellectual activity to question what they had learned.[12]

Space does not permit me to multiply case studies that demonstrate the long-term damaging effects of disallowing individual freedom to question and change religious beliefs. David Landes brings lessons from pre-Meiji Japan, China, Africa, Latin America and the Islamic nations. The contrast between affluent South Korea and starving North Korea is not merely a contrast between the results of Capitalism and Marxism, but a classic demonstration of a relationship between religious openness and economic vitality.

How does individual liberty contribute to a nation's development? Edmund Burke, one of the first British statesmen to argue for India's freedom in the late eighteenth century, stated a fundamental principle of the Industrial Revolution: "A law against property," he said, is "a law against industry."[13] He meant that if taxes are unjust, if the ownership of property is not secure, if a person cannot use his wealth as he likes, then he has little motivation to work industriously to create and save wealth.

Many leaders ignored Burke's Christian common sense, took away property rights, and condemned whole nations to poverty. The collapse of Communism at the end of the twentieth century has decisively won the argument in favour of property rights and the free market economy. However, many philosophically confused people seem to think that Capitalism is a scientific mechanism; therefore, just as a machine will everywhere produce whatever it is made to produce, Capitalism will also deliver the same results wherever it is legally established.

However, the oppression of the Russian "Mafia" in Eastern Europe since the fall of the Berlin Wall questions that belief. People are rightly beginning to suspect that perhaps the free market economy needs more than mere laws and policies. Indeed, freedom is an indivisible and organic entity. It is like a tree. You cannot demand that a tree grow only upwards, not downwards, or sideways. Freedom will either grow in all dimensions or be stifled. The various components of a free market economy: private property rights, freedom for individual initiative and enterprise, and a free market, all flow from the principles of justice and freedom of property (stewardship of God's resources) in the lives of the people. Our thoughts, opinions, ideas, conscience, talents, affections, interests, and motivations, constitute our internal property. As we shall see, a society's commitment to force or freedom springs from its core beliefs, i.e. its worldview.

Freedom of Conscience

Freedom of conscience is about every citizen's right to seek what is true and noble and discard what is false, evil, or less than noble in his life, worldview and culture. Can the freedom of conscience be separated from political and economic freedoms? Can a society have political and economic liberty without socio-religious liberty, including the right to convert?

Mature societies have recognized that socio-religious rights, such as freedom of conscience, are inextricably linked with property rights. In fact, our rights are our only true property. James Madison (1751-1836) was a Founding Father of the United States of America, its President from 1809-1817, and one of the moving forces behind the American Bill of Rights. Madison articulated the genius of the American civilization and an essence of true liberty everywhere when he explained that property is both internal and external. Real property includes whatever a person possesses and controls exclusively, namely his ideas and beliefs:

> Property. . .In the former sense, a man's land, or merchandise, or money, is called his property. In the latter

sense, a man has a property in his opinions and the free communication of them. He has a property of peculiar value in his religious opinions and in the profession and practice dictated by them ...He has an equal property in the free use of his faculties, and free choice of the objects on which to employ them. In a word, as a man is said to have a right to his property, he may be equally said to have a property in his rights.[14]

So, how does our internal property relate to our external property?

At times when I speak to primary or middle school students I ask them, "Do you study the history of India, England, or Japan?"

"Yes," they often reply.

"Do you study the history of elephants, monkeys, or peacocks?"

"No."

"Why not?"

"Because animals don't have history."

"Why don't animals have history?"

Because human beings are the only culture-creating creatures on this planet.

And what enables us to be culturally creative?

Next to language, our ideas and beliefs are our most important assets that make us creative, i.e. Creator-like. Therefore, the strength and glory of a culture depends on how strong its language is, how true its beliefs are, and how noble its ideas are. Freedom to discard what is not true and noble, and uninhibited liberty to accept what is right and good is a basic requirement to building a great culture. Freedom, thus, is the essence of creativity. A machine produces what it is programmed to produce; we create what we choose to create. Violation of individual liberty is evil because it is a violation of the Creator's image in us. Therefore, Lord Acton, the greatest historian of freedom, defined liberty as "the assurance that every man shall be protected in doing what he believes his duty, against the influence of authority and majorities, custom and opinion."[15]

Liberty has no meaning whatsoever unless it means the liberty to go against the opinion of those in power – i.e. usually the majority. Civil liberty has no meaning without religious liberty. Lord Acton, a devout Roman Catholic, who at personal cost protested against "Papal Infallibility" in defense of liberty for Protestants and others, argued that religious and civil liberty were mutually dependent. Religious liberty was secured by abridging the liberty of the state, and it was the religious liberty that made civil liberty meaningful. Acton observed that the verdict of history was that, next to absolute monarchy, democracy was the greatest threat to liberty:

> It is bad to be oppressed by a minority, but it is worse to be oppressed by a majority. For there is a reserve of latent power in the masses which, if called into play, the minority can seldom resist. But from the absolute will of an entire people there is no appeal, no redemption, no refuge but treason.[16]

Political freedom begins with individual freedom. In 1976 my wife and I left urban India to serve the poor peasants in Madhya Pradesh. To our horror we discovered that there were two sub-castes of potters in our village. One was allowed to use the potter's wheel; the other was denied the use of even this elementary level of appropriate technology. They were allowed to make only that pottery which could be made by hand. If they tried to copy the (slightly) technologically advanced sub-caste, they would be punished by the village *panchayat* – i.e. the majority! This lack of socio-economic freedom meant that they could never grow out of their poverty as long as they lived in the village and continued the profession of their caste. This oppressive social system meant that they could not contribute their best to the nation. Hence the nation was as much the loser as the families themselves.

Indian culture, like all cultures, exists because Indians are also creative: created in the Creator's image. There is, therefore, much in our culture that deserves celebration. Our art, music, dance, clothes, architecture, cuisine, epics and movies are enriching the world. Yet, there is much in our culture that is marred by the fact that we Indians, like everyone else, are sinners. As a result of sin all human creativity is mixed with evil, falsehood and oppression. We need deliverance from several traditional beliefs, values, and practices that continue to have destructive power over us.

Conversion or change of beliefs is the only available civilized (i.e. voluntary) method of social change. The strategy of Grant, Wilberforce and Ambedkar is valid today. State coercion cannot bring about social change. The only available remedy is to keep the intellectual climate of India open by allowing a free market for religious ideas. Let non-Hindu religious ideas challenge Hindu beliefs. Traditional Hinduism then will have either to defend itself or reform itself. As Jesus put it, it is truth that sets us free.[17]

Mahatma Jotiba Phule became the pioneer of the Dalit renaissance in India because he understood the relationship of truth to liberation. He called his movement *Satya Shodhak Samaj* – The Community of Truth Seekers – because he realized that to liberate a people long oppressed by socio-religious slavery, one needed to teach them to question traditional beliefs and to seek truth.[18]

Modern India's Constitution, therefore, wisely institutional-
ized the right to believe and propagate one's beliefs. It recognized every individual's freedom to choose his/her beliefs and
affirmed that a free market of ideas was more basic to liberty
than a free market in goods and services. It was an affirmation
of every citizen's only real property – the non-material, intellectual, spiritual property – that is ultimately the basis of all other
property that a person creates and owns.

Conversion and Loyalty to Community

Conversion has both negative as well as positive
dimensions. It involves rejection of some beliefs, values
and traditions and acceptance of new ones. However,
conversion is not rejection of one's family or community. But,
unfortunately, in the "fallen" world that sometimes becomes
the price of truth. The Lord Jesus and his disciples were Jews.
All the early Christians were Jews who believed that Jesus was
the Jewish Messiah (or Christ). They saw themselves as true
Jews and, therefore, continued to worship in the Jewish temple
and synagogues. However, they could not simultaneously follow Jesus the Messiah and practice untouchability. In the first
Church council in Jerusalem, recorded in Acts 15, the Jewish
disciples of Jesus Christ made a formal decision to discard untouchability and accept non-Jewish ("Gentile") believers as
equals. It was at this point that the Jewish leadership began to
treat Jesus Christ's followers as heretics – apostates, aliens, members of a different religion. In the province of Asia, where they
fled to, others began to call them "Christians" rather than Jews.
Such schisms are unfortunate, but there are times when it is
more important to follow truth and virtue than to follow a tradition, or the majority in a given community. Ultimately it is
truth that will bless both the minority and the majority.

India's greatest asset is her people. But illiteracy, superstitions, and forced labour – by-products of the caste-system – have stunted and shackled the potential of the vast majority. For example, why do so many of our women have to carry water or bricks on their heads as domestic or casual labourers? Why can't husbands or employers provide them with wheelbarrows? Their time and energy is not put to better use because our culture simply does not care for the weak and marginal. It is great to build dams, industries, "silicon valleys" and "cyber cafes." But it would be foolish not to realize that these are merely icing on the cake. As Nobel Prize winning economist Amartya Sen keeps pointing out, a more fundamental economic development of India is taking place in those slums and remote jungles where missionaries have gone to love, serve, and emancipate people. When these missionaries share with the marginalized the story of a God who loves them enough to die for them they do more for the future of India than our politicians and industrialists do. For a downtrodden tribal and "untouchable" to discover that he/she is valuable, is a brand new beginning. This beginning is indeed a threat to India's traditional culture. But it is a challenge from which – in the interest of India's future – no patriot should back off simply because the traditional Indian culture is threatening to fight back.

Hindutva and Force

If liberty is basic to nation building, why is the option of force so seductive? Practically speaking community and freedom cannot co-exist without order. If order does not come from within – from inner spiritual regeneration – then it has to be imposed from outside, by force. As Robert C. Winthrop, Speaker of the U. S. House of Representatives from 1847-49, put it,

> All Societies must be governed in some way or the other. The less they may have of stringent State, the more they

must have of individual self-government. The less they rely on public law or physical force, the more they must rely on private moral restraint. Men, in a word, must necessarily be controlled either by a power within them, or by a power without them; either by the Word of God, or by the strong arm of man; either by the Bible or by the bayonet.[19]

Philosophically speaking, freedom is not a natural part of most worldviews. It has not been a part of Hindu, Muslim, Buddhist, Orthodox, or Catholic Christian traditions. Historically the modern ideas of freedom — religious, political, economic, and press freedom — grew in the Protestant Christian struggle for liberty of conscience. The conversation between Dara Singh's friends and the journalists reported above shows that the Indian Aryans agree with Adolf Hitler that "conscience is a Jewish invention."[20] As a corollary, one of Hitler's ministers, Alfred Rosenberg, justified the Nazi's mass murders on the ground that, "Justice is what the Aryan man deems just. Unjust is what he so deems."[21]

Horrendous as these statements sound, in fact, they are logically inescapable given the worldview of the European Enlightenment. It was this worldview, often called "Secular Humanism,"[22] which produced the fruit of Fascism, Nazism, and Communism. In his important book on freedom and fascism, Prof. Veith discusses the proposition that if there is no God, human beings could not be spiritual creatures made in the Creator's image. Humans' "choice" would be nothing more than chemical responses. Conscience would then be nothing but cultural conditioning. Without an ultimate spiritual reality (God), each child would be born as a "clean" slate. Society would write on that slate, and the child would begin to hold some values as as preferable ("good") and others as objectionable ("evil"). Of itself (i.e. intrinsically), in the absence of a holy God, nothing is "good" or "bad," "just" or "unjust." "Conscience," the sense of right and wrong, as a metaphysical entity would be an illusion, or worse, a Judeo-Christian deception: a control mechanism.

Prof. Veith demonstrates that any worldview that resists a transcendent God inevitably takes away individual freedom of conscience. This is what the opponents of conversion are seeking to do in India. Freedom, justice and conscience are spiritual concepts, rooted in the belief in a Creator who is free — transcendent, i.e. beyond the cosmos. God has made humans — male and female — in his image, which includes creative freedom and the ability and freedom to make value judgements, such as the following:

Aesthetic:	"this is beautiful, that is ugly"
Cultural:	"this is noble, that is vulgar"
Moral:	"this is right, that is wrong"
Epistemological:	"this is true, that is false."

These freedoms are the essence of being creative creatures. God created nature through his Word, wisdom, knowledge and understanding. We, his image bearers, create culture similarly using language, wisdom, knowledge, and the understanding that God gives.[23] Denial of individual freedom destroys what it means to be human. It stifles our creativity, our ability to give our best to our nation and our world.

God owns each individual and all things. John Locke, the great British political theorist and exponent of civil liberty, understood that individual freedoms spring from the fact that individuals are the property, not of the state, but of their Creator:

> For Men being the Worksmanship of one Omnipotent, and infinitely wise Maker: All the Servants of

> one Sovereign Master, sent into the World by His Order, and about His Business, they are His Property, whose Workmanship they are, made to last during His, not one another's Pleasure. . .[24]

Dr. Ambedkar and the other framers of India's Constitution were right in giving freedom to the citizens of India. They bequeathed the gift of a freedom to us that was a product of the Judeo-Christian worldview; even if some of them personally were followers of the secular worldview of the French Revolution.[25] Fascism, one end result of a God-less worldview, makes citizens a property of the state. It, therefore, destroys human freedoms as it did from Revolutionary France, Fascist Italy, Nazi Germany, and every Communist country. The murder of Graham Staines is a warning that the Hindutva movement is working to replace India's freedom with fascism.

Why Does Hindutva Undermine Freedom?[26]

There are two obvious reasons why Hindutva undermines freedom and operates on the basis of force (except when restrained by national or international outcries and efforts to uphold the Constitution and the "rule of law").

First: *if truth cannot be known, race or culture must become the glue to hold a people together.* Both postmodern secularism and traditional Hinduism believe that human reason is incapable of knowing objective truth and morality. They also preclude the possibility of an infinite, personal God who exists, who knows truth, and can reveal it to human beings in rational language. In the absence of any certain knowledge of truth and falsehood, right and wrong, Hindutva has no choice but to advocate that culture and tradition should hold the nation together. It has to make all personal quests for truth subservient to the authority of "traditional Hindu culture" as defined by the changing whims of the Hindutva movement. Hindutva's core assertion is that India should be held together not by truth, morality or law, but by one minority's particular idea of a "common culture." Personal freedom and rights, especially the freedom of religion and conscience to reject some aspects of one's own culture, is obviously the single biggest threat to Hindutva's belief-system.

Second: *individual freedom and human rights are not a part of the traditional Indian culture.* Our freedom (as distinct from Independence) is a legacy of the British Evangelical movement, which was the dominant culture-shaping force in India throughout the nineteenth century. Any effort to take India back to its traditional culture has to take us back to a culture that operated on the basis of force rather than freedom. Force provides stability; freedom can be unsettling in the short run.

Many starry-eyed Indians, who are ignorant of Indian history, think that India was free before the British colonized it. The fact is that Hindu India never, I repeat *never*, knew what freedom was, until the Evangelical movement began to set us free. Many no doubt consider this somewhat extreme. But can they point to a single one-hundred-year period in Indian history when an upper caste person was free to eat with a sweeper? When was a sweeper free to become a professor or a ruler? When was a woman or non-Brahmin free to study the Vedas? When was an unarmed subject ever a "citizen," with rights to challenge the King, Prime Minister or Chief Justice in the press, or petition in court for redress of grievances without retribution, or on the streets through *satyagraha?*[27]

The rise of Buddhism is a case in point. Buddhism was what Lord Acton would have called an act of treason by a minority against the majority. Therefore Hinduism and

Islam wiped Buddhism off the shores of the sub-continent. Buddhism returned to India with Amedkar, only because Christian missions had brought freedom.[28]

Healing For The Soul Of India

The cause of missions is a battle for healing the sickness in the soul of India – the sickness that keeps hundreds of millions of our people stunted: spiritually, socially, intellectually and physically. Why must India respect a Mother Theresa or a Graham Staines only if they heal our sick bodies, and hate them when offering healing to the soul of India?

The Folly of Relativism

The foregoing is not an apology for the superiority of Western culture over Indian culture. Quite the contrary: as a preacher of the Gospel, Graham Staines was completely out of step with the postmodern Western culture whose central doctrine is "absolute" relativism of all truth and all religions. Staines became a missionary because he had rejected the folly of his own contemporary culture.

Not too long ago certain tribes in Orissa offered human sacrifices to get a good harvest from their gods. A human being who sacrifices his own (or his neighbour's) child as a sacrifice to his god has to be devoutly religious. But respect for this kind of religiosity is criminal. And to try and make a distinction between "primitive" religion and "higher" religion is deception if one has already chosen the premise that no one knows truth. Without knowledge of truth there can be no objective standards for judging anyone's religious practices as superior or inferior to another. Who could say sacrificing your money to God is superior to sacrificing your child?

In choosing to be a missionary, in riding a rickety old bicycle in a "backward" district of India, Graham Staines had turned his back on the materialism of his own culture whose highest values are personal peace and affluence. So, the discussion here is not about Indian culture versus Western culture, but between truth versus falsehood, excellence versus mediocrity, nobility versus wickedness. Staines was not a proponent of Western culture. He was preaching the Gospel of Jesus Christ, which he believed was true and had the power to regenerate and transform our souls. The following are pointers to certain truths that emerge from the witness of the Staines family.

First: We Are All Sinners

We have already noted that it is not merely the murder of Graham Staines that attests to the fact that our souls are sick. Our brothers and sisters were sick with leprosy; instead of caring for them we threw them out on the streets as "untouchables." Missionaries like the Staines sacrificed themselves to restore the dignity of our brothers and sisters, which we had violated. If it is a crime to desecrate an idol of a god, then it is sin to violate what truly is the image of God – a human being. Casteism and untouchability, oppression of women, female infanticide and foeticide, corruption, child-prostitutes, child-labourers, and illiterate children that surpass numbers in any other nation on earth testify to our sinfulness. We continue to abuse the image of God. Thus, we, one of the most corrupt nations in the world, deceive none but ourselves when we deny the fact that we are sinners.

An increasing number of the Indian intelligentsia, surfing on the temporary tidal waves of truthless relativism unleashed by postmodern education, boast that far from being sick, the Indian soul is divinity itself. Therefore, they believe that ancient India was the greatest civilization because one ancient Indian discovered the mathematical concept of zero, and another was a great surgeon! It is legitimate to take pride in our heroes. But our ancient and contemporary heroes are a proof, not of our greatness, but of our sickness. Why couldn't this head start in mathematics and medicine keep us as world leaders in science and in caring for the sick?

Some of our forefathers built a great university in Nalanda. True! It was destroyed. Also true. The question is – why was it never rebuilt? Why didn't some of our ashrams turn into colleges and universities, as did the monasteries in Europe? Imagine a great university being destroyed in England by a Napoleon: would it remain dead even after Napoleon is gone? Wouldn't a culture that believes in learning rebuild it, besides building new universities? The fact is that the Hindu doctrine of *Maya* – that the material universe is somehow unreal – and its corollary – non-rational mysticism – destroyed the very foundations of science and learning in India. As Einstein observed, science cannot even begin unless we presuppose the reality and value of the universe.[29]

There was indeed no dearth of merit or personal excellence in individual Indians. The problem has been that our sinfulness and false philosophies do not enable us to build a socio-economic-political infrastructure that would facilitate and sustain great teamwork, which a university or a department in a university, call for. Usually an individual wins the Nobel Prize because of a great team behind him. In any case, a great culture, by definition, is teamwork – the very thing our sinfulness makes difficult.

All cultures are corrupted by sin, because all human beings are sinful. India, along with the rest of the world suffers from sin – the sickness of the human soul. India's problem is compounded by the fact that *Adwaita* (Non-Dualism), the most influential of all Hindu philosophies, makes it hard for Indians to even admit that good and evil are real, and that human beings are sinful. Logically, an Advaitic Hindu, who believes that the human soul is God, cannot even admit that the murderers who burnt alive Graham Staines and his two young sons are sinners.

Second: Our Sins Deserve Punishment

Suppose the real murderers of Graham Staines cannot be prosecuted because the police mess up the case or the eyewitnesses lack the courage to testify truthfully. And imagine a perfectly plausible scenario that after their acquittal, the murderers turned "religious" heroes, go on to fight elections, win convincingly, and become ministers. What would their triumph suggest?

Prima facie the above scenario would suggest that morality is meaningless, power is what matters. For morality to be real there has to be a final moral auditing beyond this life, because the books are never fully balanced in this life. A lot of people die having lived in comfort on the strength of money extorted as bribes, stolen, or borrowed that they had no intention to repay. St. Paul said that he preaches and asks people to repent of their sins because God has appointed a day when He will judge and punish sins:

> Since we are God's offspring, we should not think that the divine being is like gold or silver or stone – an image made by man's design and skill. In the past God overlooked such ignorance, but now he commands all people everywhere to repent. For he has set a day when he will judge the world with justice by the man he has appointed. He has given proof of this to all men by raising him from the dead.[30]

Third: We Continue To Exist And Remain Accountable To God Beyond This Life.

How could a woman respond to the burning alive of her

husband and two sons with loving forgiveness for the murderers? Graham's widow, Gladys, and daughter Esther revealed their secret when they sang at the funeral:

> *God sent his son, they called Him Jesus:*
> *He came to love, heal, and forgive*
> *He bled and died to buy my pardon,*
> *An empty grave is there to prove my Saviour lives.*

> *Because He lives I can face tomorrow*
> *Because He lives all fear is gone:*
> *Because I know He holds the future*
> *And life is worth the living just because He lives.*

> *How sweet to hold a new-born baby,*
> *And feel the pride and joy he gives;*
> *But greater still the calm assurance*
> *This child can face uncertain days because He lives.*

> *And then one day I'll cross the river*
> *And fight life's final war with pain*
> *And then as death gives way to victory*
> *I'll see the light of glory and I'll know He lives.*[31]

Through this song Gladys and Esther testified to the fact to which the Apostle Paul refers in his speech in Acts 17, quoted earlier. The resurrection of Jesus Christ is proof that the ultimate reality is not death but God – the source of life.

"But the resurrection is impossible," assert the Rationalists.[32]

What arrogance! How can you know what is possible or impossible with God? You don't even know if the ultimate reality is death or God.

Even the most sophisticated philosopher cannot escape

belief in life out of death. What is ultimate: Life or Death?

It is possible to believe that death is the original and ultimate reality. But then one has already conceded that all life has come out of death. But if life is ultimate, then it is simply foolish to think that the source of life – God – cannot bring life out of death. Some of the disciples who saw Jesus die on the cross did not believe in his resurrection, even after the women who went to the grave to perform the last rites found him alive and reported it to the disciples. They accepted the fact of his resurrection only after they saw him, talked and ate with him. Thomas – the disciple who came to India in the first century – was absent when Jesus first came to the other disciples. They told him that Jesus had actually risen from the dead. Thomas still couldn't accept this "fairy tale" to be true. He said that he would not believe without verifying their claim empirically. He would need to put his finger in the holes in Jesus' hands where the nails had been driven and his hand in Jesus' side where the Roman soldier's spear had pierced him.

The resurrected Jesus came to Thomas while he was with the other disciples. The Lord Jesus invited him to verify empirically and publicly that he who had been nailed to the cross, whose death had been confirmed by the spear-thrust, and who had been buried before their eyes, had actually risen from the dead.

Thomas now had another problem. His theory was that death is the end of life. When you are dead, you are dead. That is the end. But a new set of facts confronted his intelligence now – a man who had died in front of his eyes was standing before him alive. The choice before Thomas was to either continue believing his theory that death is the ultimate reality or accept the fact standing before him. "Death is the end of human life" is only a belief born of ignorance. How do you know that death, not

God, is the ultimate reality?

Thomas realized that if Jesus had actually been raised from the dead then here was the proof that we continue to exist and remain accountable to God beyond our death. The Resurrection of Jesus Christ is the ultimate historical evidence that the moral law is as real as God himself is. Jesus, as he had prophesied before his death, died for our sins. It was not the justice and nobility of this world that had been hanging on the cross of Calvary, but the sin of the world – its injustice, wickedness and cruelty. The cross was proof that there are consequences of evil, "the wages of sin are death." Likewise, the resurrection was irrefutable evidence that a righteous God exists, and that faithful obedience has consequences – resurrection life.

Graham Staines believed in preaching the Gospel of the death and resurrection of Jesus Christ, because he knew that this message could heal the sickness of the soul of India. It is a message that gives empirical basis for belief in moral absolutes:

- sin has consequences – Jesus died because of the sin of the world
- righteousness has consequences – God raised the Righteous One from the dead.

Fourth: Sinners Can Become New Creatures

The history of evangelical revivals in the West offers irrefutable evidence that the Gospel is a redemptive message.[33] It not only gives a firm rational basis of calling good "good" and bad "bad," but it also provides a means of forgiveness and deliverance from sin. The tragedy of the European Enlightenment and rationalism is that it rejected God's Messiah and tried to find a man-centered basis for ethics, while eating up the moral capital generated by Him. Now the West has nearly exhausted its capital and has learnt that like its predecessors – including Greece, Rome, or India – it too will never find another credible basis for believing in objectively true morality. That is the basic reason why the Post-Christian West is not only catching up with the levels of immorality in our parts of the world, but in some areas it is in a suicidal rush to overtake us. World history knows of no Saviour besides Jesus Christ.

Professor Sair Singh, a Trinidadian of Indian descent and a graduate of Harvard University, now teaches Hinduism in Moscow. During a visit to Moscow in the summer of 1999 I was discussing with him the contrast between America, which impeached President Clinton because he lied about his private life, and Russia, which allowed Stalin, who killed 35 million innocent people, to die in his bed in peace. Prof. Sair Singh explained to me why the moral standards in America are much higher than those of the Russians (and Indians).

"Although the theology of the Russian Orthodox Church"[34] he explained, "is very similar to the biblical theology which shaped the American ethos, in practice most 'Orthodox' Russians do not have the same confidence about their salvation by grace alone which the biblical Christians do. The Bible teaches that we do not have to earn our salvation, because Jesus took the punishment for our sins. We need to repent for our sin and accept Jesus' death and resurrection as sufficient sacrifice for our sin. The Orthodox Russians, by contrast, perform religious rituals in order to earn their salvation. They soon discover that they are not good enough, and that they will never be good enough, because in order to survive, let alone succeed in real life, they have to compromise with evil – if not to actually use evil means. So, they give up trying to be good.

"In America, by contrast, the evangelical revivals assured the believers that they didn't have to earn their own salvation. Jesus' sacrifice had already atoned for their sin and had secured their pardon and reconciliation with God. God accepted them as his beloved children – not on the basis of their righteousness, but because of Christ's righteousness through their repentance and faith. We may fail and fall, but we can be forgiven and make a fresh start in our growth towards God's standards. This assurance of personal salvation freed the believers to continue to pursue holiness in spite of personal failures and external persecution. Moreover, faith in the resurrection and experience of the love and care of God enabled them to continue to love God, and fight against the corruption of their own society even when they suffered loss. They knew that they had an assured reward in heaven."[35]

Gladys, the widow of Graham Staines, is not perfect. But the triumph of her faith (born of her assurance of salvation), her conquest of evil by good, of hate by love and forgiveness, in the face of such tragic loss is a heart-moving authentication to the observation of this professor of Hinduism. It is clear that tinkering with political, judicial, and economic systems will not eradicate corruption from our hearts. Graham Staines preached the Gospel because he believed that the Gospel is the power that can heal our spiritual sickness. Through the spontaneous response of love and forgiveness towards those who killed their husband/father, sons/brothers, Graham's widow and daughter have exhibited the truth that the Gospel makes its believers a "new creation."

So, "Why Must You Convert?"

The answer is, because we have all sinned and must one day stand before God and give account for our every word and deed.[36] We will be condemned to hell unless we repent of our sin and accept the forgiveness that God offers on the basis of Christ's sacrifice. What hope is there for the criminal who commits a crime and also stubbornly rejects the offer of free forgiveness?

Conversion, that is, healing the moral sickness of our souls, is necessary because India's problems do not spring from inferior genes, limited intelligence, lack of resources, or overpopulation. There is no dearth of individual ability and excellence in India. It is our moral deficiency that has created a culture that prevents most of us from making the best use of our abilities for the glory of God, social good, and our own individual fulfillment. Finding a cure for the corruption in our hearts is our greatest need.

Conversion, in the biblical sense, means a transformation of our hearts and minds. It is a regeneration of souls that are sick or dead in sin. We are converted when we repent of our sin and are "born again," by the grace of God, through the power of the Holy Spirit, to become holy and beloved children of God's love. Such conversion of our souls is essential for transforming our culture.

Chapter Seven

Two Enlightenments and One Light

"Life is solitary, poor, nasty, brutish and short."
- Thomas Hobbes, pioneer of the European
Enlightenment

"Life is suffering." The First "Noble Truth"
- Siddhartha Gautama Buddha, the father of
the Asian Enlightenment

*"In this world you will have trouble; fear not, I have
overcome the world."*[1]
- Jesus the Christ, The Light of the World[2]

THREE VIEWS OF SUFFERING

The certainty of suffering – social, mental, and physical
– is acknowledged by Hobbes, Buddha and Christ.
However, the solutions to suffering are very different
from the perspectives of the European Enlightenment,
the Asian Enlightenment and the Light of the World.

Siddharta Gautama Buddha, the most influential
Indian that ever lived, saw life inherently as suffering
– *Servum dukham* ("All is sorrow"). His first Noble
Truth was "Birth is sorrow, age is sorrow, disease is

sorrow, death is sorrow, contact with the unpleasant is sorrow, separation from the pleasant is sorrow, every wish unfulfilled is sorrow – in short, all the five components of individuality are sorrow."[3] Therefore, for Buddha the only way to escape suffering was to escape life via *Nirvana* – the cessation of personal or individual existence.

The Lord Jesus said that he had come to the earth to give us abundant life,[4] not to help us escape existence. The Romans had colonized his people. He knew the indignities of slavery and oppression. Yet, he did not detach himself from the suffering of others. He shed tears over Jerusalem because sin and suffering were against the will of his Father who intended life to be good. Human beings had been created to rule over the earth, not to let it inflict pain upon them. So, the Lord Jesus confronted the root of sorrow – sin. He – the sinless one – embraced our human sin and suffering upon the cross, overcoming them by his resurrection. His brutal death, glorious resurrection and the gift of God's Holy Spirit inspired such faith and courage in his followers that they went everywhere countering the reign of evil by preaching the kingdom of God and by demonstrating its power to heal our broken world in a substantial way.

Establishing the kingdom of God in the hearts of men here and now became the antidote to evil, oppression and hunger. The Lord Jesus taught that as a small seed grows into a mighty tree, his kingdom will advance, healing suffering and conquering evil until he returns and the kingdoms of the earth become fully the kingdom of God, and the earth itself is renewed.

What does "the Kingdom of God" mean? It begins as God's rule in our hearts, which bears fruits of righteousness in all our relationships. Historically, the Kingdom of God has included increasing emancipation of the individual: (i) from private sin and corruption in public life through the reform of public life, (ii) from ignorance and superstitions through education, (iii) from natural limitations and disease through science and technology, and (iv) from religious and political tyranny through law, democracy and economic development. These have been some of the social fruits of the Gospel – of the message of Christ's death and resurrection. These results ripened most fully in Northern Europe and North America after the sixteenth century Protestant Reformation in Europe[5] and have then spread as a blessing from there to most other parts of the world.

The European Enlightenment of the eighteenth and nineteenth centuries began to secularize Western optimism, which had been a result of faith in Christ's resurrection. The European Enlightenment presumed that "Man," without God, could build his own utopia – the perfect kingdom of man. The God-less "messiahs" of the twentieth century, however, turned out to be monsters. Nazism, Fascism and the two World Wars came as the climax of God-less "Humanism." Hitler, Mussolini, Stalin, Mao Tse-Tung and other dictators, whose rise was directly linked to the impact of God-less humanism, killed over 100 million people in the last century.[6] They shattered the West's secularized optimism, paving the way for an acceptance of Buddha's escapist Nirvana by some of the intellectual elite.

THREE VIEWS OF KNOWLEDGE

The views of suffering differ between the two Enlightenments and the Light of the World, because they begin with different theories of knowledge. The biblical worldview implies that the human mind can know truth because God has revealed it to us. The European Enlightenment assumed that human reason could know truth independent of revelation. The Gnostic[7] Enlightenment was built on the assumption that truth could only be known by transcending rational thought through a mystical experience.

Buddhist Mysticism

Following Greek and Upanishadic Gnosticism, Buddha thought "Ignorance" (Avidhya) was the root of creation. As *Paticca-samuppada* or the "Chain of Dependent Origination" put it:

> Out of Ignorance arises Imagination, thence Self-consciousness, thence Name and Form (i.e. corporeal existence), thence the Six Senses [the sixth being Thought], thence Contact, thence Feeling (or Emotion), thence Craving, thence Attachment, thence Becoming, thence Rebirth, and thence all the manifold ills that flesh is heir to.[8]

Since the creation, including the human body, self-consciousness, and rationality, was a product of cosmic "Ignorance," Buddha sought a mystical enlightenment that sidestepped rationality, sought to eliminate self-consciousness and to escape the body as well as the world.

Buddhism spread from humble *caityas* or sacred spots, which were small groves, (sometimes a single large tree) outside a village or town. These were popularly revered as abodes of elemental spirits or genii. Some of them grew into *viharas,* which were both monasteries and temples. A few of them developed into great institutions of Buddhist learning. For example, the Nalanda "university" at its peak is said to have had as many as a thousand teachers! These monasteries and universities lacked neither brilliance nor dedication. Yet, they did not develop any continuing tradition of science, medicine, technology or economic and political principles of progress and freedom, and therefore did little to minimize human suffering.

Why?

The answer is: because Buddhism started with the assumption that both physical reality and human rationality are products of Ignorance (*Avidhya*). Therefore, the enlightenment it sought was to transcend rationality by altering consciousness and finding mystical knowledge and occult power. Unlike Christian universities in Europe the Buddhist monasteries and universities did not aim at cultivating the mind to understand and master the external world. Scholars wonder whether it was Buddhist distrust of rational knowledge that eventually made it too weak to withstand the ninth century intellectual offensive of revived Hinduism under Adi Shankaracharya. An equally important question is: Why were not enough Indians willing to shed their blood in defense of great institutions like Nalanda, when the Islamic onslaught by relatively small numbers of non-Indians began to drive Buddhism out of India? Was it because people considered these institutions useful only for the monks' nirvana, but irrelevant for social progress?

Historians would no doubt give contradictory answers. Yet, it has to be noted that this aspect of Buddhist history repeated itself in the twentieth century when Communism began its armed offense against Buddhism in countries like China, Tibet and Cambodia. Some scholars feel that laymen and women closed their eyes to the suffering of the monks, because for centuries the monks had closed their eyes to the suffering of the world, to find the bliss within their own altered state of consciousness.

Christianity, Revelation and Rationality

The more important question is: Why did the Judeo-Christian tradition[9] use rationality and creativity (instead of mysticism and "transcendental" meditation[10]) to lead the fight against suffering, against the violation of human liberty and dignity?[11]

The answer is: the Bible begins with an assumption that is opposite to Gnosticism and Buddhism. It teaches that the creation is a result of God's wisdom, not ignorance. The Lord Jesus was the *Logos* – the Word, Wisdom, or the Reason of God – who created the universe.[12] The Apostle Paul asserted that "in Him (Jesus) were hidden all the treasures of wisdom and knowledge,"[13] because he was "the visible image of the invisible God."[14] The Bible emphasized that men and women were created in the image of the Creator.[15] This implied that to be godly included becoming rational and creative like God, and to be opposed to evil and injustice, which were and are the result of human disobedience to God.

So, the West's confidence that the human mind could know truth came from the assumptions that God was Truth, and that he wanted us to know the truth. This He had revealed to us through His works (nature), through His Word (the Bible), and most fully through the Lord Jesus. It was up to us to receive the Truth and to use our minds in order to establish His reign and be good stewards of this earth.

The Rise And Collapse of the European Enlightenment

It is necessary to understand the rise and collapse of the European Enlightenment to understand modern India, including various approaches that the Dalit revolution has taken.

The European Enlightenment retained Christian confidence in human rationality and creativity to fight against evil and suffering. But at first it downplayed divine revelation and later excluded it altogether. While the biblical assumption was that human reason was *necessary* to know truth, the Enlightenment thinkers assumed that human reason (without divine revelation) was *sufficient* to know all truth. This was the heart of the humanist hubris referred to earlier. It produced Thomas Paine's *Age of Reason*, which, in turn, gave birth to the Age of Ideology.

Early Enlightenment thinkers such as Descartes (1596-1650) and Locke (1632-1704) believed that human reason could know all truth – including the truth about God. Berkeley (1685-1753) doubted if we could know for sure if the external world existed outside our mind. David Hume (1711-1776) demonstrated that the human mind alone could not know God.

Does that then mean that God does not exist? Or does it mean that human reason is limited? Some Enlightenment thinkers decided to stick with the finite mind and give up faith in God. So, instead of studying God, they began studying man – and God-less "Humanism" was born.

Immanuel Kant (1724-1804) went on to demonstrate that the human mind could not know reality as it really is. We can only "know" what appears to us. We could not even know right and wrong in any absolute sense. Kant's philosophy raised questions regarding the very idea of objective truth.

Sigmund Freud (1856-1939) and his followers mounted the next offensive against rationalism by demonstrating that it is not merely God that the human mind could not know; it could not know itself. This is because the bulk of our mind is sub-conscious and irrational, which can only be probed partially through psychoanalysis, dream analysis, *et cetera*.

In spite of this increasing debunking and the weakening of the *Age of Reason*, popular faith in rationalism persisted. Science, it seemed to many, was still solving the riddles of nature. However, after Heisenberg's (1901-1976) "Uncertainty Principle" (1927) won general acceptance, the scientific community itself began admitting that, beyond a point, the structure of the universe does not correspond to the structure of human consciousness.[16] The human mind, therefore, can never know the truth. God-less western intellectuals had finally arrived at the starting point of the Upanishadic and Buddhist sages: That non-rationality, rather than rationality, was the ultimate principle in the universe! This ushered in what Francis Schaeffer called the West's "Age of Non-Reason."[17]

Ample research and documentation exists to show that the Reformation – rooted in Biblical revelation – gave birth to the seventeenth century's science, medicine, technology, democracy, and capitalism, which produced the modern world. For example, Sir Isaac Newton's secular admirers still criticize him for spending more time studying the Bible than nature. For every one word he wrote on science, Newton wrote four on the Bible. The prophetic books Daniel and Revelation were his favourite parts of the Bible.

While human rationality (submitted to biblical revelation) created modern Western civilization, the Enlightenment's Rationalism (separated from revelation) culminated in Fascism and Communism. It was also the basis of the existential despair of the 1950s; the anti-ideologies of the hippies of the 1960-70s who prostrated at the feet of gurus, god-men and tantrics; and finally California's "New Age" of superstitions of the 1980s-90s.

The foregoing extremely brief sketch of the intellectual history of the West in the last five hundred years will, I hope, help us understand the worldview options available to the victims of Hinduism today.

ALTERNATIVES TO HINDUISM

Brahminism, (i.e. orthodox Hinduism), maintains that the indignity and suffering endured by the lower castes is God's will for them because God made them from his feet to serve the upper castes. The lower castes are also reaping the just consequence of their "bad karma." Brahmins (like the Pharisees of Jesus' day) believe in external religious "purity." Therefore, for an upper caste person, the touch or even the shadow of the lower castes is "contaminating." (But beating, raping, exploiting, or even murdering a Dalit is non-polluting!)

The Light in India

Untouchability and caste are not God's will but social sins, taught William Carey (1761-1834), in stark contrast to the Hindu idea. It was this British cobbler-turned-missionary (along with Grant) who many historians credit with having laid the foundation of India's modernization. What makes us impure, Carey said, is to insult human beings by labeling some as "untouchables" and "Shudras." As we shall see in the next chapter, it was through Carey's work in Bengal[18] that India's darkness – philosophical, social and moral – began to be challenged by the Light of the World.

Western missions and the Indian Church have often appeased Brahminism and displeased lower castes. Yet the fact remains that it was Christian missions, with their influence on Indian leaders like Raja Ram Mohun Roy (1772-1833) and Jotiba Phule (1827-90), which triggered India's social reform movements. These, together with the missions-led education revolution supported by British rule, resulted in India's nineteenth century "renaissance."

Mahatma Phule and the European Enlightenment

Mahatma Jotiba Phule, the pioneer of the lower caste revolt in India, is a good illustration. He studied in a Scottish Mission school in Poona and was so profoundly influenced by Christ that he extensively celebrated the Lord Jesus as the "Baliraja" (the Sacrificed King).[19]

Unfortunately, however, during the nineteenth century some servants of the East India Company brought the atheistic humanism of the European Enlightenment into India. Enlightenment thought appeared attractive because it vigorously championed many Christian values: e.g. liberty, human rights, hope for a better life, confidence that we can know truth, and so on. However, at a deeper level, the Enlightenment undermined Christianity and led many Indians down a blind alley. One of the most tragic losses for India's poor and oppressed castes was that the writings of Thomas Paine confused Mahatma Phule. Just as the Enlightenment led Europe to "endarkenment," so also it proved impotent to lead Phule's followers into the liberty they sought.

In the fourteenth chapter of his book, *Slavery*, Mahatma Phule acknowledged that some Brahmins gave him the works of Thomas Paine to wean him away from Christ and to motivate him to fight against British rule. They misled him, teaching that caste was not a part of Hinduism, therefore all Hindus needed to unite and fight against the British. As a result Mahatma Phule started taking lessons in *Dand Patta*, a kind of swordplay or fencing. It was only as he matured that he realized that India needed Christ, as well as the British, for learning elementary things like patriotism. Phule wrote,

> The enlightened [Brahmin] people have proved this favourite thesis of theirs on the authority of quotations from the works of celebrated authors like Thomas Paine and others. Being misled by the motivated propaganda of these 'enlightened' Brahmin scholars, I acted in a misguided way in my boyhood. But when I reflected long and deeply over the teachings contained in the above mentioned books, the true meaning of the motivated propaganda of these 'enlightened' Brahmin scholars

dawned on me. If all the Shudras regard themselves as the co-disciples of the second Baliraja (Jesus Christ) we would, then, be constrained to condemn the spurious books (and scriptures) of the ancestors of the Bhats [Brahmins]. Their arrogant arrogation of superiority to themselves over the other Shudras would be exposed and their idle priestly class will not be able to fatten itself at the cost of the Shudras. Then even the (all-powerful) Brahma (or even his sire) will not dare claim the superiority of the Bhats over the Shudras. The original ancestors of those people did not know even the meaning of the word 'Patriotism'. So it is not surprising if they have interpreted the word 'Patriotism' in such a queer way.

Even before the advent of Baliraja [Jesus Christ] the English took lessons in patriotism from the Greeks [sic].[20] After their conversion to Christianity [the religion of Baliraja] they imbibed this virtue of patriotism to such an extent, and perfected it so much, that no other people [nation] could equal [or excel] them on the score of patriotism. Perhaps one may bracket them with George Washington, the follower of Baliraja [Jesus] in America. If you do not want to compare the English with such great leaders, then you may compare them with Lafayette, the French follower of Baliraja [Jesus]. That would be a logical comparison. If the original ancestors of these enlightened Brahmin scholars were truly patriotic, then they would never have inscribed articles [or enactments] in their [religious] books condemning their own compatriots as worse than beasts. How strange it is that these Brahmins consider themselves as pure [elevated, ennobled] when they eat the droppings and drink the urine of beasts [cows] that consume human excreta, but refuse to drink the water of a fountain from the hands of a Shudra![21]

As Mahatma Phule realized that the Brahmins were promoting the writings of the Enlightenment thinkers like Thomas Paine to turn Shudras against Christ, he became wary of their game plan. He began urging Shudras to follow Christ. Nevertheless, the poison of atheistic Rationalism took its toll without Mahatma Phule becoming fully aware of it. He urged the Shudras to seek truth. But how do we know truth? Mahatma Phule seems to have accepted the Enlightenment idea that the human mind without divine revelation could know truth.

Dr. Ambedkar and Buddhism

Mahatma Phule's successor, and the twentieth century's leader of the depressed classes, Dr. Bhimrao Amedkar, was better able to see the inherent weakness and tragic consequences of such humanist arrogance. Having earned two doctorates, one from New York and the other from London, he could not trust the humanist *Age of Reason*. Phule was a great soul, but Ambedkar's education was more complete. He belonged to a generation of statesmen who saw the humanist hope of utopia blow up in mushroom clouds over Nagasaki and Hiroshima. Therefore, to him, as with many other Western intellectuals, Buddha's pessimistic perception seemed more accurate: life *is* suffering; man is incapable of knowing truth or building utopia. So in 1956, with over 300,000 followers, Baba Saheb tried escaping Hinduism through Buddhism – the Asian path to Enlightenment.

Buddhism seemed attractive because, at a superficial level, it was something of a revolt against Brahminism. It also had the advantage that it was an Indian alternative to Hinduism. Baba Saheb was disappointed that the light of Christ had not adequately transformed the Indian church. Many upper caste converts to Christianity brought their caste prejudices into the Church. In order to become upwardly mobile, the lower caste converts tended to distance themselves from members of their own earlier castes. Some shortsighted missionaries compounded the problem by accepting only the upper caste children in their educational institutions. This was partly because the upper-castes had the money to pay fees, and also because some missionaries feared that if they admitted children from the lower castes then the upper castes would not send their children to Christian schools.

It was not as though the Gospel was not challenging India's darkness. One of *Shivaji's* descendents, and the most important leader of the Depressed Classes Federation before Dr. Ambedkar, was Sahu Ji Maharaj. He had supported Dr. Ambedkar's studies and prepared the way for him to become the leader of the depressed classes. Sahu Ji Maharaj repeatedly admitted that Christ introduced the idea and practice of human equality to modern India. Here is one of the formal edicts of Sahu Ji Maharaj issued to his state in Maharashtra:

His Highness earnestly desires that the educational bodies receiving help will follow the good example set by the American Mission at Miraj, and the good example set in the St. Xavier's and Wilson Colleges and Mission School in Bangalore, Panchgani and Arya Samaj schools, colleges and gurukuls where no difference is made between the touchable and untouchables.

Charitable institutions are meant for poor people and even the poorest untouchable human being has a right to be treated on a footing of equality. His Highness earnestly hopes that his medical staff will follow the good example set by the foreigners, especially the American Mission at Miraj.

Be informed that in all public buildings, charity houses,

state homes, public Government inns and river watering places, public wells, etc. no difference on account of caste to any human being is to be taken account of, just as in Christian buildings and as Doctors Vanless and Gail in the American Mission treat all with the same love, so also here they are to be treated as not esteeming any unclean.[22]

In spite of the fact that it was the Light of the World that began the emancipation of the lower castes, many leaders of the lower castes are still attracted to Buddhism primarily because it enables them to retain the benefits of "Reservations" in government schools, colleges and jobs. They know that the Reservation also brings indignity and stigma with it, but they don't see many alternatives.

As one who comes from Buddha's own Sakya community and as one who reveres Dr. Ambedkar, it is hard for me to admit that historically Buddhism has never proven to be a sufficient antidote to Hinduism. Kanshiram, the man behind the present social ferment in India, reached this conclusion before he founded DS4 and the Bahujan Samaj Party. He started out with a Buddhist Research Foundation, but felt that Dr. Ambedkar, his intellectual guru, had placed unjustifiable confidence in Buddhism. Rightly or wrongly Kanshiram felt that political power might be more effective in liberating the oppressed than Buddha's way, which included giving up his political kingdom.

It should not be difficult for anyone to understand why Scheduled Caste or "neo-Buddhism" is a poor substitute for Scheduled Caste Hinduism. Neo-Buddhism necessarily brings caste into Buddhism, thereby making Buddhism merely another sect of Hinduism. One cannot take the benefit of being a lower caste and avoid its stigma. The uncomfortable fact that we have to face is that even original Buddhism failed to counteract Brahminism. For now, however, let us get a clearer perspective on the options available to those seeking salvation from the social sins of Brahminism.

Dr. Ambedkar did not follow Jotiba Phule into a Western "humanist" Enlightenment. Nor did Kanshiram follow Dr. Ambedkar into Buddhist Enlightenment. Each of them saw the limitations of his predecessor's choice. Kanshiram's committed followers[23] have also become disillusioned with his political path to salvation. Therefore, many are now reconsidering Ambedkar's path. This phase of uncertainty, I hope, would cause careful readers to take a fresh look at Dr. Rochunga Pudaite's journey into liberty at the end of this book.

Christ and India

To me it is obvious that (in spite of all the failures of Western missions and the Indian Church) the Light of the World is the only demonstrable hope for the oppressed in India. My book, *India: The Grand Experiment*, is a detailed demonstration that India's freedom is a fruit of the Christian Gospel, not a result of Mahatma Gandhi's work. It examines how individual, intellectual, economic, press and political freedoms came to us during the nineteenth and twentieth centuries. That book, however, does not explore the difference between those who followed Dr. Ambedkar into Buddhism in Maharashtra and those who chose Christ in Mizoram, Nagaland, Meghalaya, Manipur and other places.

I am not aware of any comparative scientific study of the social effects of conversion to neo-Buddhism and Christianity in India. Such a scientific study is required — and not merely to satisfy the curiosity of social scientists. It is needed to enable the leaders of *bahujan samaj*[24] to make careful choices. No responsible leader would want to lead his followers on a path that would be regretted by later generations.

From my personal observation I know that the quality of

life that Jesus has given to his followers is incomparably higher than what the Buddhist Enlightenment has done. A tiny state such as Mizoram, in spite of its problem with insurgency, has become the most literate and the least corrupt state in India. Hindu officers testify that while it is a nightmare to conduct a peaceful, orderly election in a Hindu majority state, it is a pleasure to conduct an election in Mizoram. There are no homeless Naga or Mizo beggars in their states. In fact, beggars go to obviously resource-poor states like Nagaland and Mizoram from resource-rich states like Bihar. In terms of child welfare, female literacy, crime rate, average lifespan and other socio-economic indices used to measure quality of life, the states in India that have significant Christian populations are beginning to draw the experts' attention and admiration.

Our myopic media cannot see beyond Chandra Babu Naidu, the present Chief Minister of Andhra Pradesh, as an explanation for all the good things that are happening in Andhra Desam. Without downplaying the significance of Mr. Naidu's personal contribution, which I admire, please allow me to assert my belief that a careful socio-historical study will demonstrate that the mass conversions to Christ in the middle of the twentieth century in Andhra Pradesh is a key factor why AP is surging ahead of the northern states. Faith in Christ is one of the competitive advantages of Andhra's Dravidians over the Aryans of the cowbelt (where Christians constitute less than 0.1% of the population).

Social scientists do not usually undertake the kind of research we need because they tend to assume that religious differences have no significant socio-economic impact. Amartya Sen, Nobel laureate in welfare economics, however, does acknowledge that it was Christianity that made a difference in states like Mizoram and Kerala:

Advances in basic education have often come from forces that have railed against traditional politics (including protests against the historical hold of caste practices), or against traditional cultures (sometimes in the form of missionary activities). While the latter may explain the higher achievement in elementary education in say, Goa, or Mizoram, Kerala has had the benefit of both types of breaks (education-oriented lower-class movements as well as missionary activity). . . [25]

For admitting such facts Amartya Sen has paid the heavy price of being attacked viciously by the Vishwa Hindu Parishad (VHP). Brahminism cannot tolerate truth.[26] The problem, however, is not merely that the VHP is too bigoted to look at the obvious facts. Often social scientists themselves lack humility to learn from the father of their discipline – Max Weber. States like Mizoram, Kerala, and now Andhra Pradesh are significant evidence that the core of Weber's thesis was correct: the Protestant Reformation was the source of the socio-economic success of Northern Europe. So it should not be surprising that Christ's light is now also brightening up the dark corners of the Indian sub-continent, just as it is transforming Latin America, parts of Africa and the Far-eastern Asian countries like South Korea.

Demonstrably, the Lord Jesus is the greatest liberator of the downtrodden in India. That is one reason why every well-wisher of India must examine Christ.

European Enlightenment and Education as Salvation

Mahatma Phule is my hero. We come from the same caste group. He was a *Mali* (gardener); I am a *Kushwaha* (vegetable grower). Following the European Enlightenment Phule assumed that human reason would be sufficient to know truth and thus deliver us from the superstitions and slavery of Brahminism. He, therefore, looked at education as salvation. The irony is that he had ample evidence, and he wrote about it himself, that British secular education was in fact reinforcing Brahminism's hold over India. In his Memorial Address to the Education Commission (1851) he complained, "One of the most glaring tendencies of Government system of high class education has been the virtual monopoly of all the higher offices under them by Brahmins."[27]

Phule could not have foreseen that the recommendations of the Educational Commission would begin the university movement in 1857, which by 2001 would be so firmly under Brahminical rule as to start teaching Vedic Astrology! In his book *Slavery*, Phule had castigated astrology as one of the chief means of India's enslavement by Brahmin priests.

So, although Phule could not have foreseen the future, he did know that it was not rationalism or education that had abolished the British slave trade two decades before he began his campaign against "slavery" in India. The British slave trade was only abolished because of the stirrings of Christian conscience and many decades of self-sacrificing work by thousands of people led by men like MP William Wilberforce.

Mahatma Phule should not be blamed because other brilliant men like Thomas Paine also did not realize that they were sawing off the branch on which they were sitting. They wanted the social fruit of the Gospel without its root beliefs.

Take, for example, the idea of human rights. It was Paine's advocacy of human rights that attracted men like Phule to him. Mahatma Phule wanted India to be a society that gave equal rights to all castes. What Phule did not know was that Paine's *Rights of Man* made sense only against the background of French theologian Theodore Beza's (1519-1605) work, *Rights of Magistrates*, (written almost two centuries before Paine), and the

Constitution based on the security of the Magna Carta (1215).

Beza was John Calvin's successor and leader of the Reformed Churches in French-speaking Europe. His understanding of the rights of magistrates came from the Bible. He argued that the magistrates were servants of the kingdom, not of the king. The king's own servants were only his cooks, cleaners, gardeners and guards. These were obliged to obey the king because they had voluntarily entered his personal service. Not so the magistrates who had accepted a civil office to serve society. The king was only the first among equals. The king, magistrates (i.e. lower officials) and the people were all subjects of Christ, who had brought God's kingdom to this earth. So, if a king's orders were unjust and contradicted God's law, the magistrates had the right to disobey the human king, because the magistrates were obliged to obey God before obeying the king.

The Magna Carta (1215) is the foundation of modern constitutions including those of the UK, the USA and India. To secure the Magna Carta, King John and his barons swore on Oath before God that every person would obtain justice, even if the King himself, or the Chief Justice, or any official (e.g. Prime Minister) breached any clause of that Charter. The fear of God, the Judge of the entire world, and of eternal judgment is the foundation of our rights under these Constitutions.

How could an upper caste mob, supported by a Member of Parliament, District Magistrate and Superintendent of Police totally disregard the constitutionally guaranteed fundamental rights of Dr. Maurya and myself? (see Chapter One) The explanation is that without Theodore Beza's theological framework of the Kingdom of God, a District Magistrate is nothing more than a lackey of his political boss! Without the fear of God and eternal judgment, "human rights" are nothing more than a piece of paper to be dispensed or withheld at the pleasure of rulers.

Mahatma Phule dedicated his book against *Slavery* to:

> The Good People Of The United States, As A Token Of Admiration For Their Sublime Disinterested And Self-Sacrificing Devotion In The Cause Of Negro Slavery: And With An Earnest Desire, That My Countrymen May Take Their Noble Example As Their Guide In The Emancipation Of Their Shudra Brethren From The Trammels Of Brahmin Thralldom.[28]

Phule was impressed by the fact that some white Christians, because of their beliefs and values, had taken up arms against fellow white men to liberate blacks from slavery. It is disappointing enough that his "Earnest Desire" that his countrymen take up the battle for emancipation of Brahminism's slaves has not yet been fulfilled. What would make Phule turn in his grave is that now, as a result of the influence of God-less humanism and commercialism, even America is turning its back on the idea of fundamental rights. How can millions of Americans become so heartless as to murder their own babies in their mothers' wombs? How can they even think of producing embryonic babies for the sole purpose of harvesting their stem cells?

It should surprise no one that the monster of racism is re-emerging in "civilized" nations like England. The post-Christian West – without a Christian revival – is destined to become the world's first post-human civilization. The Caucasian conscience is becoming as insensitive as the Aryan conscience in Germany. It has to, because if human rights are rooted in nothing more than human reason or human will, then they will necessarily change at the whim of rulers – a ruling Brahminical elite in India, or a ruling pro-abortion majority in

America. Human rights are "inalienable" or "fundamental" – beyond the rulers' ability to bend them at will – only if they come from beyond men, from God.

Mahatma Phule, Pandit Jawarharlal Nehru and Indian novelists like Mulk Raj Anand,[29] following Thomas Paine, put their hopes in education to lead India to truth, human rights, and emancipation. As early as 1851, when the "enlightened" British controlled education, Phule was already sensing that education might not lead to liberation. Today, under the reign of a Brahmin physicist Murli Manohar Joshi, India's minister for Human Resource Development, that hope is getting dimmer by the day.

The oppressed in India do need world-class education for their emancipation. Christian institutions need to find creative ways of raising finances to subsidize their education. The phenomena of modern mass education as well as modern higher education are both products of the Light of the World.[30] Therefore, to be effective in a wholesome way, education has to be undergirded by the truth and values of the Gospel.

Asian Enlightenment and Human Rights

How can we trust that the human mind can know truth? This can be assumed only within the context of the biblical worldview: that the ultimate reality is a personal, rational God who created the universe. Without that presupposition, Buddha, not Phule, makes greater philosophical sense.   Dr. Ambedkar, therefore, was right in not trusting Phule's rationalistic path to Enlightenment. However, what he overlooked was that (a) Buddhism was not a radical enough alternative to Brahminism, and that (b) Buddhism was even less capable than God-less Rationalism to serve as a source for human rights.

Buddhism has been a dominant cultural force in many

countries like Sri Lanka, Burma, Tibet, China, Korea, Thailand, and Japan. But nowhere has it produced a society that values human rights.

Rather, Buddhism oppresses minorities whether in Tibet, Sri Lanka, Myanmar or Japan. The Buddhist Sinalhese majority in Sri Lanka has denied the Tamil labourers their rights to language, culture and equal opportunity. The Buddhist majority in Myanmar (Burma) brutally suppresses the minority tribes. Buddhism was powerless to prevent Kampuchea's (Cambodia's) Communist government from killing one-third of its own population.

The roots of this phenomenon are not hard to understand: Buddhism does not breed human rights because it does not value human individuality. Far from being valuable, according to Buddhism, human individuality is our metaphysical problem; naturally Buddhism cannot and will not value individuality. Although the short-term benefit of Reservations makes Buddhism attractive to the Dalits, in the long run the notion of human rights goes completely against the presuppositions of Buddhism.

This is not to deny that some later schools of Buddhism believed in the existence of the individual soul. Yet, the dominant belief in Buddhism has been that selfhood is a delusion caused by cosmic Ignorance. Even those schools that acknowledge the existence of the individual soul think that human individuality is the human problem.

From its inception Buddhism has maintained that the universe has three salient features: it is full of sorrow (*dukha*), it is transient (*anicca*), and it is soulless (*anatta*). The doctrine of *anicca,* or transience, means that there is no permanent individual being, with dignity and rights. Just as a chariot is nothing but a particular arrangement of wood and metal, so is a human being nothing but a compound of five psycho-somatic elements: Body, Feelings, Perceptions, States of Mind, and Awareness. These change from moment to moment. There is no permanent substratum to them. An old man is not the same entity he was seventy years before as a child. There is no "be-ing," only becoming. The only thing permanent about the universe is its impermanence or flux. The notion of permanence is a product of primeval ignorance out of which spring all sorrows. This low view of individuality makes Buddhism an attempt to lose one's notion of individuality. Its goal is not to find or restore one's dignity and liberty.

Gautam Buddha did not see Buddhism as an alternative to Hinduism, but only as a "Middle Way" between the extremes of the asceticism of monks and the indulgence of the average Brahmin priest. That is one reason why Brahmins did not persecute Buddha. During the reign of king Ashoka (273-232 B.C.) Brahmins began to lose some of their political power to Buddhist monks. This resulted in persecution under Hindu king Pushyamitra Sunga. Sunga destroyed many Buddhist temples. Serious persecution continued in the sixth century when the Huan king Mihirakul destroyed monasteries and killed monks (about a thousand years after Buddha). In the seventh century persecution intensified under Sasanka, the fanatical Saivite king of Bengal.

Eventually Hinduism stifled Buddhism by adopting Buddha as the ninth avatar[31] of Vishnu. In the absence of a reliable, authoritative, liberating Word of God, Buddhism succumbed to priest-craft and superstitions. Buddha did not believe in God, but Buddhist priests made him a god. All forms of idolatry, as we saw in an earlier chapter, preclude the notion of objectivity of truth. And without truth, there is no liberty.

In many ways Dr. Ambedkar was ahead of his times. Today the intellectual climate is more ripe for mystical anti-intellectualism than it was in 1956. The Age of Non-Reason, or what I call the New Age of Superstitions, is drawing many converts from the sterile God-less Rationalism of the European Enlightenment. The enormous success of movies like *Crouching Tiger, Hidden Dragon* suggests that millions today are keen to explore occult knowledge: the power of "mind over matter." The irony is that no civilization has exerted greater power of mind over matter than Western civilization. It acquired that power, not through secret meditation techniques, but through humble, open, observable, verifiable and reproducible experimentation. We in India will condemn ourselves to a few more generations of ignorance, perversion, exploitation, and slavery if once again we turn *en masse* to a failed mystical tradition.

God-less Rationalism deprives us of our dignity by reducing us first to the status of monkeys and then to a bio-chemical machine. However, Buddhism does not provide any higher view of human dignity. It is the Light of the World that informs us that we have the glory of being made in our Creator's own image. We lost our dignity of being God's children because we sinned. We rebelled against our Father. When we believe in Jesus Christ's incarnation, death and resurrection, God gives us his Holy Spirit and restores that dignity.

The Basis For Human Dignity

My Muslim friends object to the idea that God became man in the person of Jesus Christ. The idea seems repulsive to them because it does not befit the majesty of Allah. They ask: "Can God become a dog?"

I usually respond with a counter-question: Imagine that the Queen of England is visiting New Delhi. She is given a red-carpet welcome. The streets are lined up with flag-waving crowds. Her entourage is being escorted by the "Who's Who" of the Delhi *durbar*.[32] Now imagine that from the corner of her eye the Queen spots a leprosy patient, a beggar, with a hungry, sickly baby sucking at her dry breasts. The Queen stops her limousine, gets out, walks to the beggar, and picks up the baby in her arms!

She has violated all protocol. But has she deprived herself of her majesty? What if the Queen proceeds to donate her blood for the baby? Would she be violating her dignity or adding to the dignity of the child? Undoubtedly, the event and the child would be front-page news all around the world.

Can the Queen donate her blood for a dog? She might be willing to, but their blood would not match. God became man, because man was made in His own image. His coming to us did not deprive him of his majesty; it restored our dignity.

"How valuable is a human being to God?" I ask my Muslim friends.

Obviously God cares enough for us to send us his prophets. Through them he tells us what to do and what not to do. We disobey one prophet, he sends another; we refuse to listen to the second, and he sends us a third. And then . . . ?

I have two daughters: suppose one of them gets into bad company, gets involved with drugs and the mafia, gets sucked into a maelstrom of her own making. Her life is endangered. What will I do? Will I just send her e-mails and faxes, telling her what to do and what not to do?

She has already disobeyed everything her mother and I have taught her. Now, what are my options? How valuable is she to me? Will I keep sending her instructions, or will I, at some stage, go myself and do whatever I can to rescue her from her situation, even if it costs me my life?

How can I, a selfish, sinful human being even contemplate the option of sacrificing my life for her?

I can do so because I am made in the image of God who loves me enough to come to this world of sin and sorrows, and to take my sin and suffering upon himself. He died so that I may have life – godly, abundant and eternal. His death defines the value of a human being – our true value.

* * *

We do not need to spend incarnation after incarnation meditating to find our salvation. The Lord Jesus Christ has already paid the penalty of our sin.

You can find forgiveness for your sins and become a child of God. Repent for your sin and accept the Lord Jesus Christ as your Saviour and Lord. Then join with others who genuinely wish to come under his lordship and become creative, rational fighters together against indignity, slavery and poverty as servants of his kingdom.

Meet together with other followers of the Lord Jesus to worship, pray, and study; to share abilities, and life's material goods and blessings, as well as its problems and challenges. Work towards extending God's rule on earth, elect wise leaders, and do the good works God has uniquely prepared for you. Share this good news with others in your family and community. Help them also find this true Freedom and Dignity that only comes through the Lord Jesus, who said, "*I am the Way, the Truth, and the Life.*"[33]

Chapter Eight

The Light and the Birth of Modern India

Imagine a quizmaster at the finals of the All India Universities' competition. He asks the best-informed Indian students, *"Who was William Carey?"*

All hands go up simultaneously.

So, he decides to give everyone a chance to answer. The audience is asked to judge which answers are correct.

"William Carey was the botanist," answers a Science student, "who discovered a new species of Sal-tree in Bhutan, named *Careya* after him by Dr. Roxburg. Dr. Carey was the first to specialize in the Indian flowers of the Amaryllidaceae family, one of which is named after him.

"Carey brought the English daisy to India and introduced the Linnaean system of gardening. He also published the first books on science and natural history in India such as the three-volume *Flora Indica*, because he believed the biblical view, 'All Thy works praise Thee, O Lord.' Carey believed that nature is declared, 'good' by its Creator; it is not *maya* (illusion) to be shunned, but a subject worthy of human study. He frequently lectured on science and tried to inject a basic scientific presupposition into the Indian mind that even lowly insects are not 'souls in bondage,' but creatures worthy of our study."

"William Carey was the first Englishman to introduce the

steam-engine to India at the Serampore Mission Press, and the first to make indigenous paper for the publishing industry," pipes up the student of **Mechanical Engineering**. "Carey encouraged Indian blacksmiths to make indigenous copies of the steam-engine."

"William Carey was the missionary," announces an **Economics** major, "who first introduced the concept of a Savings Bank to India, to fight the all-pervasive social evil of usury. Carey believed that God, being righteous, hated usury, and thought that lending at the rate of 36-72 percent interest made investment, industry, commerce and the economic development of India impossible."

"The moral dimensions of Carey's economic efforts," the student continues, "have assumed special importance in India, since the trustworthiness of the Savings Banks has become questionable, due to the greed and corruption of the bankers. The all-pervasive culture of bribery has, in many cases, pushed the interest rates up to as much as 100 percent, and made credit unavailable to honest entrepreneurs."

"In order to attract European capital to India and to modernize Indian agriculture, economy, and industry, Carey also advocated the policy that Europeans should be allowed to own land and property in India. Initially the British Government was against such a policy because of its questionable results in the United States. But by the time of Carey's death, that same Government had acknowledged the far-reaching economic wisdom of his stand. Our own Indian Government too, after one-half century of destructive xenophobia, has again opened the doors for Western capital and industry."

"William Carey was the first man," asserts a **Medical** student, "who led the campaign for a humane treatment for leprosy patients. Until his time they were sometimes buried or burned alive in India because of the belief that, 'A violent end purifies the body and ensures the transmigration into a healthy new existence, while natural death by disease results in four successive births, and a fifth as a leper.' Carey believed that because Jesus in his love touched and healed leprosy patients, they should be cared for humanely"

The student of **Printing Technology** stands up next. "Dr. William Carey is the father of printing technology in India. He brought to India and then taught and developed the modern technologies of printing and publishing. He built what was then the largest press in India. Most other printers had to buy their fonts from his Mission Press at Serampore."

"William Carey," responds a student of **Mass Communications**, "was a Christian missionary who established the first newspaper ever printed in any Asian language because Carey believed that, 'Above all forms of truth and faith, Christianity seeks free discussion'. His English-language journal, *Friend of India*, was the force that gave birth to the social reform movement in India in the first half of the nineteenth century."

"William Carey was the founder of the Agri-Horticultural Society in the 1820s, thirty years before the Royal Agricultural Society was established in England," contends a post-graduate student of **Agriculture**. "Carey did a systematic survey of agriculture in India, wrote for agriculture reform in the journal, *Asiatic Researches*, and exposed the evils of the indigo cultivation system two generations before it collapsed."

"Carey did all this," adds the agriculturist, "not because he was hired to do it, but because he was horrified to see that three-fifths of one of the finest countries in the world, full of industrious inhabitants, had been allowed to become an uncultivated jungle abandoned to wild beasts and serpents."

"Carey was a Bible translator, who was the first person to translate into English and publish great Indian religious classics such as the *Ramayana*, and philosophical treatises such as *Samkhya*," says the student of Literature. "Carey transformed Bengali, which was previously considered 'fit only for demons and women,' into the foremost literary language of India. He wrote Gospel ballads in Bengali to bring the Hindu love of musical recitations to the service of his Lord. He prepared Bengali dictionary and grammars, and wrote the first Sanskrit dictionary for scholars, including Greek and Hebrew synonyms."

"Carey was a British cobbler," joins in the student of Education, "who became the first professor of Bengali, Sanskrit and Marathi at the Fort William College in Calcutta where the civil servants were trained. Though he himself only had some home schooling till age 14, Carey began dozens of schools for Indian children of all castes and launched the first vernacular college in Asia at Serampore, near Calcutta. Without any formal education, Carey taught himself six European languages. He and his assistants then translated parts or all of the Bible into more than 40 Indian languages. He wanted to develop the Indian mind and liberate it from the darkness of superstition. For nearly three thousand years India's religious culture had denied to most Indians a free access to knowledge. The Hindu, Mughal, and British rulers had gone along with this high caste strategy of keeping the masses in the bondage of ignorance. Carey displayed enormous spiritual strength in standing against the Brahmin priests and their vested interests in depriving the masses of the freedom and power that comes from knowledge of truth."

"William Carey introduced the study of Astronomy into the Subcontinent," declares a student of **Mathematics**, "He cared deeply about the destructive cultural ramifications of astrology: fatalism, superstitious fear, and an inability to organize and manage time.

"Carey wanted to introduce India to the scientific culture of astronomy. He did not believe that the heavenly bodies were 'deities that governed our lives'. He knew that human beings are created to govern nature, and that the sun, moon, and the planets are created to assist us in our task of governing and keeping time. Carey thought that the heavenly bodies ought to be carefully studied since the Creator had made them to be signs or markers. They help divide the monotony of the universe, of *space* into directions — East, West, North and South — and of *time* into days, years, and seasons. They make it possible for us to devise calendars and measure time to microseconds; to study geography and history; and to plan our lives, our work and our societies. The culture of astronomy sets us free to be rulers, whereas, the culture of astrology had made us subjects — our lives determined by the stars."

A post-graduate student of **Library Science** stands up next. "William Carey", she reveals, "pioneered the idea of lending libraries in the Subcontinent."

"While the East India Company was importing shiploads of ammunition and soldiers to subdue India, Carey asked his friends in the Baptist Missionary Society in England to load educational books and seeds into those same ships. He believed that would facilitate his task of regenerating the Indian soul and soil and of empowering the Indian people to embrace ideas that would generate freedom of mind. Carey's objective was to create indigenous literature in the vernacular. However, he believed that until such indigenous literature was available, Indians needed to receive knowledge and wisdom from around the world to catch up quickly with other cultures. He wanted to make worldwide information available to Indians through lending libraries."

"William Carey was an evangelist," maintains the student from the Indian **Forest Institute**, "who thought that 'if the Gospel flourished in India, the wilderness will, in every respect, become a fruitful field.' Therefore, he became the first man in India to write essays on forestry, almost fifty years before the government made its very first attempt toward forest conservation in Malabar. Carey both practiced and vigorously advocated the cultivation of timber, giving practical advice on how to plant trees for environmental, agricultural and commercial purposes. His motivation came from his belief that God has made man responsible for the earth. It was in response to Carey's journal, *Friend of India*, that the government first appointed Dr. Brandis of Bonn to care for the forests of Burma and arranged for Dr. Clegham to supervise the forests of South India."

"William Carey," argues a feminist, a **Social Science** scholar, "was the first man to stand against both the ruthless murders and the widespread diabolical oppression of women, virtually synonymous with Hinduism in the eighteenth and nineteenth centuries. The Hindu male in India was crushing the female through polygamy, female infanticide, child marriage, widow-burning, temple prostitution, euthanasia and forced female illiteracy, all in the name of 'religion'. The British Government had timidly accepted these social evils as being an irreversible and intrinsic part of India's religious mores. Carey began to conduct systematic sociological and scriptural research. He published his reports in order to raise public opinion and protest both in Bengal and in England. He influenced a whole generation of civil servants who were his students at the Fort William College to resist these evils. Carey opened schools for girls. When widows converted to Christianity, he arranged marriages for them. It was Carey's persistent battle against Sati (widow burning), for twenty-five years, which finally led to Lord Bentinck's famous Edict in 1829, banning one of the most abominable of all religious practices in the world."

"William Carey was an English missionary," pronounces a student of **Public Administration**, "who, initially, was not allowed to enter British India because the East India Company was against the conversion of Hindus. Therefore, Carey worked in the Danish territory of Serampore. Later, however, because the Company could not find a suitable professor of Bengali for the Fort William College, he was invited to teach there. During his professorship lasting thirty years, Carey transformed the ethos of the British administration from indifferent imperial exploitation to that of a 'civil' service."

"By policy the East India Company did not interfere with the socio-religious practices of their subjects in India, however evil they were. On the other hand, Indians influenced their British rulers. The idolatry, the 'women of easy virtue', the Nawabs, and the colony's wealth, combined to create havoc with the morals of the British officers. Carey, being a missionary and not a ruler, put up a determined and persistent opposition to this corruption. He also imparted a religious spirit of gentleness, and a missionary spirit of service to the administrators. His influence in transforming the British administration is often considered greater than that of the legislative work of the Governor-Generals from Cornwallis to Bentinck."

"William Carey", reflects a student of Indian Philosophy, "was a preacher who revived the ancient idea that ethics and morality were inseparable from religion. This had been an assumption underlying the Vedic religion. But the Upanishadic teachers separated ethics from spirituality. They thought that the human self (*Atman*) was the divine Self (*Brahma*). Therefore, our spirit could not sin. Our *Atman* only gets deluded and begins to imagine itself as distinct from God. What we require is not deliverance from sin but enlightenment, which is a direct experience of our 'divinity.' This denial of human sinfulness and emphasis on the mystical experience of our divinity made it possible for us in India to be intensely 'religious' yet at the same time unabashedly immoral.

"Carey began to affirm that human beings were sinners and needed both forgiveness for sin and deliverance from its power over them. He taught that it was not ignorance but sin that had separated us from God; therefore, it was impossible to please God without holiness. According to him, true spirituality began only when we repented for our sin. This teaching revolutionized the nineteenth century religious scene in India. For example, after Raja Ram Mohun Roy, one of the greatest Hindu scholars of the nineteenth century, came in contact with Carey and the other missionaries at Serampore, he began to seriously question the spirituality then prevalent in India. He summed up his conclusions thus:

> The consequence of my long and uninterrupted researches into religious truth has been that I have found the doctrine of Christ more conducive to moral principles, and better adapted for the use of rational beings, than any other which have come to my knowledge.

A student of History stands up last. "Dr. William Carey is the father of the Indian Renaissance of the nineteenth and twentieth centuries. Hindu India had reached its intellectual, artistic, architectural, and literary zenith by the ninth century A.D.. After the Absolute Monism of Adi Shankaracharya began to sweep the Indian subcontinent the creative springs of humanity dried up, and India's great decline began. The material environment, human rationality, and all that enriches human culture became suspect. Asceticism, untouchability, mysticism, the occult, superstition, idolatry, witchcraft, and oppressive beliefs and practices became the hallmark of Indian culture. The consequent invasion, exploitation, and the resulting political dominance of the foreign rulers made matters worse.

"Into this chaos came Carey and initiated the process of India's reform. He saw India not as a foreign country to be exploited, but as his heavenly Father's land to be loved and served, a society where truth, not ignorance, needed to rule. Carey's movement culminated in the birth of Indian nationalism and of India's subsequent independence. Carey believed that God's image was in man, not in idols; therefore, it was oppressed humanity that ought to be served. He believed in understanding and controlling nature instead of fearing, appeasing, or worshiping it; in developing one's intellect instead of killing it, as mysticism taught. He emphasized enjoying literature and culture instead of shunning it as *maya*. His this-worldly spirituality, with as strong an emphasis on justice and love for one's fellowmen, as on love for God, marked the turning point of Indian culture from a downward trend to an upward swing. The early Indian leaders of the Hindu Renaissance such as Raja Ram Mohun Roy, Keshub Chandra Sen and others, drew their inspiration from William Carey and the missionaries associated with him."

So, *who was William Carey?*

Well, he was the pioneer of the modern missionary movement of the West; a pioneer of the Protestant Church in India; and the translator and/or publisher of the Bible in forty different Indian languages. Carey was an evangelist who used every available medium to illumine every dark facet of Indian life with the light of truth. He is the central character in the story of India's modernization.

***

Note: This chapter is taken from *The Legacy of William Carey: A Model for the Transformation of a Culture* by Vishal and Ruth Mangalwadi, published by Crossway Books, Wheaton, Illinois (A division of Good News Publishers); 1999.

Chapter Nine

Has India Died?
...And Is A Hindu Nation Coming To Birth?

Note: This invitation to a Prayer Conference was sent to the friends of the author. About 60 people came together to pray for two days for India and Indians. The seeds of this book were planted during that conference.

Vishal Mangalwadi
May 01, 2001

> *Operation West End is the frightening story of the death of India's last "sacred cow": the Defence establishment. It is...enough reason to lose all hope in the idea of India.*
>
> Tarun Tejpal, Editor-in-Chief,
> Tehelka.com in his essay *Sleaze,*
> *Senseless Greed And Dirty Heroes.*

Recently, some Indian journalists created a fictitious company, "West End", to sell a non-existent weapon to the Indian Army. Their aim was to examine the extent of corruption in the Defence establishment. The Army had been believed to be better or less corrupt than other branches of the Indian Government. Just a decade ago, Nani Palkhivala, one of India's legal luminaries, had described the Army as one of the "best gifts" of the British [Evangelicals] to India. Unfortunately, the investigative journalists found that without an actual weapon to sell and on the strength of bribes alone, they could get into the residence of India's Defense Minister and to the President of the ruling Hindu nationalist party – the BJP. Their hidden video cameras caught many of the high and mighty taking bribes and bragging about their corrupt control over India.

Nearly a hundred hours of video footage, filmed clandestinely, convinced Tehelka chief editor Tarun Tejpal that the British idea of a civilized "India" had died. The leadership of the Indian Army had now become as corrupt as it was in the eighteenth century under Clive and Hastings, before the British Evangelicals dared to challenge and to start reforming it.

Tejpal's dejection needs to be understood. Some intellectuals had hoped that if the politicians and Hindu "activist-saints" made a further mess of India, the Army would be able to step in as the saviour!

Pravin Togadia, the "International" General Secretary of the Vishwa Hindu Parishad (VHP or the World Hindu Council) has declared that "India" is for the "unpatriotic." A new geo-political concept – *"Bharat"* – is being birthed for those who feel for the Hindu culture. Unlike modern democratic India, the new nation of "Bharat" will not be built on the strength of its intrinsic merit. It will be birthed by force. The VHP has declared its intention to train a militia of 300,000 Hindu youth to deliver "Bharat" from the hands of those who cling to India – that is, Free Marketeers, Secularists, Muslims, and Christians, *et cetera*.

The BJP/NDA[1] government's National Council of

Education Research and Training has decided that it will replace secular "leftist" history books – such as those written by Romila Thapar – with textbooks that promote *Hindutva*[2] ideology as the foundation of this new nation.

What would the above mean besides demolishing more mosques, burning Bibles, and "eliminating" more missionaries? On May 2, 2001 the Indian Army began a massive "dress-rehearsal" in the deserts of Rajasthan to prepare "Bharat" for a nuclear war with Muslim Pakistan. This could be the inevitable contribution of Hindutva to the Indian sub-continent!

It is ironic that, historically, Hinduism had so weakened the Hindu states that Muslims had no problem enslaving and ruling over them for seven centuries. Muslim rule was followed by British rule over most of these states from 1757 to 1947. To unify these states into India was indeed a British idea. British evangelicals and Western missions laboured for a century and a half to create a modern, civilized, democratic India. (See the author's book, *India: The Grand Experiment*).

British (and, later, Indian) God-less "humanists" hijacked the Christian vision for India. They believed in the doctrine of social evolution and thought that India would only become better, even without the Gospel of Jesus Christ.

The Tehelka scandal is another nail in the coffin of the God-less humanist dream of a great India. Notwithstanding the fact that Western missions have made plenty of mistakes in India, it is clear to us that India has no hope apart from the Gospel of Jesus Christ. More than that... there is yet hope for India, and that hope lies in the Gospel.

The Prophet Ezekiel was in captivity in Babylon when he was given the vision of the valley of dry bones.

Almighty God asked him, "Son of man, can these bones live?"[3] Ezekiel was not sure, because resurrection had not been a part of human history up to his time.[4] We, however, have no excuse for not believing. And if we believe, we have no excuse for not praying and working.

As a first step, therefore, we invite all those who share our belief that God's heart as well as plan is to bless India and the Indian sub-continent to join us in a summer prayer conference ...

Looking forward to seeing you,

Vishal & Ruth Mangalwadi

PS: September 2001

As events unfold in India and the world we need to continue to pray for the nation and the people of India. If you would like to join in praying for God's blessing on India and the Indian sub-continent please contact us. We will put you on our e-mailing list so that you will receive points of praise and for prayer to make your praying for India more specific and accurate.

Write to: SAR@SouthAsianResources.com

Afterword

The Shadow of the Untouchable
by
Dr. Rochunga Pudaite

My tribe in southern Manipur did not treat others as untouchables. We were headhunters until two generations ago. No wonder even the British avoided us – let alone other tribes and castes. As a matter of fact my tribe – the Hmars – were not even listed as a tribe by the Government of India, until I appealed directly to our Prime Minister, Pandit Jawaharlal Nehru. One consequence of this isolation was that although caste is *the* defining feature of most of Indian society, I knew nothing of its power until one afternoon of 1952, at the University of Allahabad.

As a student in Jorhat (1946-49) I had swept floors, cleaned toilets, and happily worked in the gardens to pay for my room and board. My parents and Christian mentors had taught me that all work was honourable, better than begging. So I never imagined that a sweeper was different from me or my fellow students . . . that is not until about 4 o'clock that fateful day. A classmate of mine and I were walking home to our hostel. Our hostel sweeper was walking a little ahead of us. The winter evening sun cast his long shadow on us. I didn't even notice it but my friend did. He suddenly flew into a rage. "You *Bhangi*!" he screamed at the sweeper, "You scum of the earth! Are you blind? Your shadow fell on me. You have polluted me!"

Until that moment I did not even know that this classmate of mine was a Brahmin! I knew him only as a good student, from a respectable family, embodying our dreams for a new India. But he abused the man, who was bigger than himself, in language that I had never heard. It was too foul to repeat.

Asserting his superior status, the Brahmin young man ordered this much older, trembling and crestfallen sweeper to lie face down. Then he kicked him as he cursed. Since I could not stomach this, I rolled up my shirt sleeves and decided to grab the Brahmin and throw him to the ground. Just then four boys appeared and shouted, "If you touch the Brahmin we will give you a lesson worse than the one he is giving to the sweeper."

I froze in shock. The Brahmin, enpowered by the support of these (enlightened!) university students, demanded of the poor sweeper, "Pay for my trip to the Ganga for purification." The sweeper begged for forgiveness and promised to pay whatever the Brahmin wanted.

Deeply troubled, I walked to my room alone. One agonising aspect of this shameful episode was that the sweeper, my classmate and I were a part of a Christian hostel – Holland Hall! Christianity that I was familiar with in North East India had liberated my tribe from our traditional inhumanity to fellow human beings. But here, in Uttar Pradesh, both the Christian as well as secular institutions of higher learning had clearly failed to humanize Hindus. The Brahmin felt he had been polluted by a sweeper. I felt that his Brahminism had polluted an institution meant to reform India. I bolted my room and poured out my soul to God, "Dear God, if you are a loving God, why do you allow a human being – your child – to be treated as the 'scum of the earth'? Lord, why, why, why can such a thing happen in this civilized and beautiful country of India? The Bible says that you love that sweeper so much that you sent your Son to die for his salvation. Even our constitution has now declared equality for all citizens. Why Lord, why then do you allow such despicable treatment to be meted out to another citizen?"

I wept before God. I was grateful that I was a Christian. I felt sorry for my Brahmin friend whose eyes had been blinded by Satan and whose conscience was corrupted by his culture. I felt sorry that his self-esteem was so shallow that he would take umbrage at a mere shadow; his purity was so phony that it could be polluted by a passing shadow. But more than that, I was sorry that I was too weak to do anything to help either the sweeper or the Brahmin find liberty from their slavery. I asked God to enable me to someday do something to help my countrymen find the liberty that he had brought to me and my people.

* * *

I grew up in a remote mountain village of Senvon in Manipur. My ancestors worshipped rivers, mountains, rocks, stars, the moon and the sun. Evil spirits constantly troubled and frightened us. Our priests were forever busy sacrificing chickens, goats and pigs to appease the angry spirits. Then one day a mail runner brought a copy of a book for my village chief. *The Gospel of John*, one of the books of the Bible, was written in the Lushai (Mizo) language using the Roman alphabet. The Chief knew it had a message but he could not read. A traveler who passed through our village could read the words, but could not understand the meaning of the message in the book. On the back page he found the address of the sender, Mr. Watkin R. Roberts.

Chief Kamkhawlun sent messengers to Aizawl (capital of what is now Mizoram State) to bring the sender of the book, Mr. Watkin R. Roberts, to his village and explain the meaning of the message in the book. Mr. Roberts approached Colonel Locke, the Superintendent of the Lushai Hills district, and asked him how to visit Senvon in Manipur. Colonel Locke told him, "The Hmar people are the most savage headhunting people in the world. They will lop off your head and have a great celebration over your dead body. When we go there we take at least 50 soldiers to guard us. I cannot spare even one for you."

Mr. Roberts, a Christian businessman from Wales, found a few young men in Aizawl to travel with him as his guides. After seven days of trudging the 100 miles over rugged mountain trails they reached Senvon. This was in 1910. Mr. Roberts met with the Chief and the village people. At first no one was interested in his stories. Then on the fifth evening he read to them a verse from the Gospel of John. "For God so loved the world, that he gave his only begotten Son, that whosoever believes in him should not perish, but have everlasting life."[1] What finally turned on the lights for my people was his illustration, drawn from their own experience of how their tribal wars were settled. Two tribes had been warring against each other for several years. Then one of the tribes decided that they wanted peace. They sent a message by beating their huge war drum on the mountaintop nearest the enemy camp. The other tribe responded by beating their drum before sundown. The tribe who first beat the drum brought a goat to the boundary of the two tribes. The two Chiefs and their men arrived at the boundary, which had been carefully drawn. They sacrificed the goat and let the blood flow across the boundary line. The two Chiefs then put their hands on the sacrificial animal and the spokesmen from both tribes discussed the terms of the peace. As soon as they reached an agreement the two Chiefs embraced each other over the slain animal. Then spokesmen pronounced peace. The people who had been at war against each other embraced, the peace restored. They were set free from their animosities and insecurities. The illustration had come right out of our tradition. It made great sense.

Mr. Roberts explained to our Chief that man was created in the likeness of God - good, happy and free. Satan deceived and enslaved man. Man ran away from God and lost his likeness to God. Becoming more like Satan he started committing crimes against God and neighbours - oppressing, if not murdering fellowmen, violating women, detroying families, robbing property and indulging in all kinds of greed, envy and immorality. God sent prophets and priests to show them the way to harmonious living, personal happiness and eternal life. But men could not change their ways. Ultimately, God took the form of man and revealed Himself to show His love, His plan of salvation and eternal happiness with Him in heaven. Jesus became the sacrificial "lamb of God" and shed his blood so that we may have peace with God and be reconciled to one another.

My father was a teenager when he heard the story of Jesus, of God's sacrifice on the cross to make peace with us – his enemies. My father gave his life to Jesus so that Jesus became his Saviour. Four other young men also decided to embrace God's message of salvation. Roberts left Senvon with a promise to return and open a school and a medical clinic to help them. But upon his return to Aizawl, Colonel Locke served him with an expulsion order to leave the Lushai Hills for disobeying orders and for "demeaning the high British culture" by sleeping in tribal homes and eating tribal food. Roberts was never again allowed to return to preach the Gospel to the Hmar people. My father and his friends learned to read the Lushai language, in order to memorize the Gospel of John, and then preached the Good News of salvation to our people.

My grandfather, who was the Chief before Kamkhawlun prior to being deposed by the British, was furious that his son had become a follower of the "white man's religion." My father was banished from home. Later he and his friends were arrested, whipped and imprisoned by the British rulers. Most Indians who have been told that the colonial rulers wanted to convert us will find it incredible and incomprehensible, but it is true that the British rulers burnt the bamboo churches my father had built, and banned taking freewill offerings to support pastors. But Jesus, who suffered for our salvation, gave power to my father and his friends to persevere. The story of Christ's death and resurrection and their personal experience of Christ gave them hope, joy, and peace. The more they were persecuted the faster Christianity grew among the Hmar people. One of their leaders, H. K. Bawichhuaka joined Mahatma Gandhi's freedom movement. He was arrested and jailed in Silchar and Jorhat until India's independence. On the day of India's independence the Hmar people also gained freedom. They assembled, burned the British edicts and celebrated independence with the dignity of being citizens of a free country.

When I was ten years old, I too accepted Jesus Christ as my Lord and my Saviour. My parents sent me to the nearest upper primary school to study — 96 miles away from my home in Churachandpur. Their aim was not so that I may get a good job and provide them with financial security in their old age, but so that "You may translate the Bible for us." To get to the school I had to walk through dense forest, infested with tigers, bears, and wild elephants. After I finished middle school I went to Jorhat, about 300 miles from home. There I worked as a sweeper, cleaner and gardener in the Mission Compound to pay for my room and board.

After I finished high school I decided to go to Calcutta to study at St. Paul's College. With Rs.150, borrowed from my relatives, I went to Silchar and boarded a train for Calcutta. When I reached the Sealdah station, before the train had fully stopped, a coolie[2] came into our compartment, picked up my luggage and ran out. I chased him through the crowd. I was afraid of all the strangers at the train station. The coolie put my luggage on a *tonga*.[3] I gave him a few coins and he left. The tongawallah asked me where I was going. He was polite and friendly. I told him, "St. Paul's College in Amherst Street." The tongawallah drove me out of the train station. The horses ran, and ran, and ran. In the darkness of the night we drove into a dark alley and stopped. The tongawallah pulled out a long sharp dagger and said, "Give me all your money or this dagger will go through your heart." Even as he pressed the dagger to my chest, I emptied out my moneybag for him. He dumped my luggage on the road and drove away. This, my first experience of mainland India, was more frightening than meeting a tiger in the jungle.

After they left I prayed to God, my heavenly Father, to guide me. I thanked him for sparing my life. I picked up my luggage, put it on my head and walked to the street without knowing where I was going. I was afraid of talking to anybody. About two hours later I saw the signboard, "St. Paul's College." I asked the *darwan*[4] to show me the Principal's house. In the morning I met Principal Eddy and told him my predicament. He was a kind Indian, educated in Oxford. He told me that the Indian Government had recently set up scholarship funds for tribal students and that I should apply for a scholarship. I went to the office and got provisional admission.

I filled out the scholarship form and, with great expectations and a prayer, sent it to Delhi. Two weeks later a letter came from the Ministry of Education saying my tribe, the Hmar, was not included in the Schedule (list) of tribes of northeast India. I was denied the scholarship. My world seemed to crumble before my eyes. I went to my hostel room and cried before God, asking Him for mercy and grace. Then I opened the Bible and read "With God all things are possible." I took my pen and wrote a long letter to Pandit Jawaharlal Nehru, Prime Minister of India, telling him about my encounter with the tongawallah, the denial of my scholarship application by the Ministry of Education, and my need of financial help to begin my college education. I assured him that I belonged to a bonafide tribe called Hmar. Ten days later I received a letter from the Prime Minister's office that a scholarship had been arranged for me and that the Ministry of Education would send the money to the college. I was overjoyed. I thanked God that I was born in India and pledged to be a loyal and worthy citizen until I died. This was 1949. Thousands of refugees from East Pakistan[5] filled the streets of Calcutta. I volunteered and helped distribute food, medicine, and clothing to the refugees. Helping and comforting people in their hour of such need lifted my own spirit.

After I finished my Intermediate Arts degree course in Calcutta I decided to transfer to Allahabad University in the heartland of India. I was hoping that I might have the opportunity to meet Pandit Nehru at his family home there and also study Hindu philosophy under Professor Kaul, economics under Professor Sanyal and political science under Professor Tewari, whose books I had read in Calcutta with great admiration. By the grace of God, a few months after I arrived in Allahabad, I met Pandit Nehru and his daughter Indira Gandhi at Anand Bhavan. They invited me to come to Delhi and introduced me to Kaka Sahib Kallelkar, Chairman of the Scheduled Castes, Scheduled Tribes and Other Backward Classes Committee. During my visit to Delhi I submitted the name of my Hmar tribe along with the Paite, Gangte, Vaiphei and other tribes in Manipur to be included in the list of tribes. I was so proud of being an Indian, of belonging to a country with leaders big enough to meet with little-known people like me and care enough to meet the needs of the minority people. I could not think of another nation more generous and caring.

In paranthesis I may add, that it was this sense of gratitude and loyalty to India that made me accept without any hesitation a dangerous assignment from Mrs. Indira Gandhi. In 1975, Ambassador T. N. Kaul came to my home in Wheaton, Illinois to ask me to work as an "Un-named Peace Emissary," to meet with Mr. Laldenga, leader of the Mizo Revolutionary movement and prepare a "Formula For Peace" in Mizoram. During the two years I spent on the mission I had three close calls. The first was when the Indian Army suspected me of being a member of the MNF guerillas; second, when a monsoon landslide carried me away in a car; and third, when an MNF operative pressed a loaded revolver to my chest, demanding "How can you say you are not a spy for India?" Working for peace was a dangerous and expensive mission. I did not bill a single

Rupee of my expenses to the government except for the Air Force helicopter I had to requisition on three occasions. It was my way of saying thank you to the Motherland for her investment in my college education. No sacrifice was too great for my country and my God. I received my reward when in the year 2000 Mizoram was declared "the most peaceful state in the union."

To continue the story of my journey into liberty and dignity, a few months after my unforgettable encounter in Allahabad, I read a book, *Christ's Way To India's Heart* by Bishop J. Waskom Pickett. There he related the story of Dr. Bhimrao Ambedkar's attraction to Christianity, but eventual decision not to follow Christ.

In 1935, Dr. Amberkar confided to Bishop Pickett, "When I read the Gospels, the Acts of the Apostles, and certain passages of St. Paul's epistles I feel that I and my people must all be Christians, for in them I find a perfect antidote to the poison Hinduism has injected into our souls and a dynamic strong enough to lift us out of our present degraded position, but when I look at the Church produced by Christian Missions in the districts around Bombay, I have quite a different feeling. Many members of my own caste have become Christians and most of them do not commend Christianity to the remainder of us."[6]

Dr. Ambedkar's remark pierced my heart deeper than the dagger the Calcutta tongawallah pressed to my chest. I know the teaching of Jesus Christ is "a perfect antidote to the poison" Satan has injected into human souls of all races: black, brown, yellow and white. It is an indictment of my failure and the failure of other followers of Christ to live a Christ-like life, as the world expects to see in us, I confessed to God. I asked God to forgive me and to help me to walk closer to him. I knew I was not perfect. I had failed the sweeper and also allowed my Brahmin classmate to continue in his slavery to a system that had so weakened our Motherland by dividing us into warring castes and tribes.

I needed Jesus to invade and rule my soul, so that I too may take up my cross and resist sin and evil even to the point of death. I knew that the Lord Jesus who had conquered death and risen from the grave to save us from our sin would help me serve my country. As I look back over my life, he did answer my prayer. He took me out of the remote mountain village of Manipur and made me a world citizen, able to play a small, yet significant role making a difference in the lives of others in the following ways.

My secular education at the university was not sufficient to equip me to translate the Bible into Hmar. So I prayed and asked God to make it possible for me to study the Bible and theology in the United Kingdom or the United States of America in order to fulfil my commitment to my father. God answered my prayers sooner than I had anticipated. Four months after my graduation from Allahabad University I was in Glasgow, Scotland studying Greek and Hebrew. I began translating the Bible. Soon I was offered a scholarship to go to the United States for further training in Biblical theology.

A few months after I arrived in America I read a book, *My India, My America* by Krishnalal Shridharani who also wrote a beautiful book *War Without Violence*, an analysis of Mahatma Gandhi and his techniques. In *My India, My America* Krishnalal narrated the story of Dr. Ambedkar's brilliant career, his painful humiliation and climactic rejection by upper caste Hindus in Baroda and his decision to become a Sikh or Buddhist. No pain is more excruciating as humiliation and rejection by one's own society. Again, I said to myself, "When I return to India, God enabling, I will do something for the untouchables."

I returned to India in 1958, with my newly translated Hmar New Testament. Until then my people had to make do with a "second-hand" translation of the New Testament from the Lushai (Mizo) language. Now, with my education in English and the original languages of the Bible and the help of Hmar elders like "Dr." Thanglung, I had been able to bring home a Hmar New Testament we could all be proud of. It was published in 1960 and became the Hmar best-seller: The first 5,000 sold out in six months. My father's dream was finally fulfilled.

After three months at home I decided to travel across the hills of Manipur, Mizoram and Assam and retrace some of my youthful life. I found that there was only one government school among the Hmar villages of the Manipur hills. My people wanted to read the Bible that God had enabled me to translate for them in answer to my parents' prayers. They needed schools. God helped us to begin nine village schools and a high school. Within 10 years God had enabled us to open 85 schools – this without any help from the government. As a result, now 85% of the Hmar people know the joy of reading and writing. They have been liberated from illiteracy, superstitions and dependence upon others. They have been set on a course where they could develop their potential, serve God and their Motherland. We sought to instill a spirit of self-reliance and the pursuit of excellence in the hearts of our students. Over the years God rewarded our labours as we saw our graduates become ambassadors of India, Chief Secretaries of the states, a Director General of Police, I.A.S. officers, doctors, lawyers, engineers, professors, pastors, and even evangelists – ambassadors of the King of Kings. Among the Hmar names you might recognize are: N.T. Sangliana, Karnataka State Director General of Police; L. Keivom, High Commissioner to New Zealand; and L.T. Pudaite, ambassador.

My conviction that Jesus is what India needs grows stronger when I consider a district, such as Allahabad, which has been one of the greatest centres of political power in India, having given independent India Prime Ministers like Pandit Nehru, Lal Bahadur Shastri, V. P. Singh, Chandrashekhar and even our present Minister for Human Resource Development, Mr. Murli Manohar Joshi. Even such districts are still oppressed by the evil of caste, and have not been able to make 85% of their population literate. That is inexcusable.

Be that as it may, our schools naturally led to a college – Sielmat Christian College. One of my deepest regrets in life is that we had close it down. We made the mistake of accepting a small financial grant from the government. That enslaved us to petty bureaucrats who had no idea of the liberating power of the Bible. They demanded that we stop teaching the Bible to all students. That was a condition that we could not accept. It was the very source of our liberty and dignity. Without the Bible we would be simply another despised Scheduled Tribe. Because of the Bible we became rapidly advancing children of God. Instead of surrendering our liberty to bureaucrats and petty politicians we closed down the school after eight years of outstanding achievements. God-willing, in the near future we hope to launch a world-class national institution of higher learning particularly for India's Scheduled Tribes and Scheduled Castes.

Looking back, I am extremely grateful for what God has done for me and for others through me. He saved me from the sins that arise from living outside God's control. He became my Father. I was poor, but I did not have to envy others or beg from them. My Father has showered His love upon me. His care and His provision have been sufficient for all my needs. He has made my life useful not merely for my Motherland but in over one hundred countries. I have flown over 30 lakh[7] miles to serve people all over the world. I have seen greed and grief among the nations which no human being is able to erase. We need the dynamic of the teaching of Jesus Christ which, Dr. Ambedkar observed, is "strong enough to lift us up out of our degraded position."

Notes

Foreword by Mr. Ram Raj, I.R.S.

1. Indian Revenue Service
2. The British Government's Simon Commission drew up an official list ("schedule") of the socially depressed castes and tribes in 1930. These are known as Scheduled Castes (SC) and Scheduled Tribes (ST). A quota is reserved for these castes and tribes in government schools, colleges and jobs, which has made a significant difference. Many SC and ST families have progressed beyond other castes that were socially superior to SC & ST. These are now known as Other Backward Castes (OBCs).
3. A case in point is the 1996 massacre at Bathani Tola, Bihar. See "Ajay Singh, Curse of the Castes", *Asiaweek*, Sept. 18, 1996. (http://www.asiaweek.com/asiaweek/96/1018/is1.html)
4. Literally, the reign of Ram, the Hindu avatar of Vishnu, who is the hero of the epic *Ramayana;* a golden age in the past

Chapter 1: What Enrages Dr. Maurya?

1. A person of the fourth or the lowest caste. In this book I will often include "*Ati-Shudra*" or the totally untouchable (outcaste) within the category of Shudra. The four castes are: *Brahmins* (Priests), *Kshatriya* (warriors), *Vaishya* (merchants), *Shudras* (serving classes.)

These are subdivided into over 6,000 castes.

2. The British Government's Simon Commission drew up an official list (Schedule) of the socially depressed castes and tribes in 1930. These are known as Scheduled Castes (SC) and Scheduled Tribes (ST). A quota is reserved for these castes and tribes in government schools, colleges and jobs, which has made a significant difference. Many SC and ST families have progressed beyond other castes that were socially superior to SC and ST. The latter are now known as Other Backward Castes (OBCs). Some Shudra castes are also called Middle Castes since they had acquired land and political power after the decline of the Mughal Empire in the eighteenth century. Dr. Maurya belonged to the *Jatav* caste, a sub-caste of *Chamars* or leather-workers.

3. Town's name has been changed. It is located in central India.

4. Hindutva is an attempt to indiginize European fascism. It seeks to organize India around "Hindu culture" rather than India's constitution. The core of the Bharatiya Janata Party (BJP) is the political face of Hindutva.

5. The Reservation System was begun by the Government of India as an affirmative action programme in educational institutions and the civil service to give a leg up in society to the lower castes that had been discriminated against for millennia.

6. Bhartiya Janata Party (BJP); the Hindu party that leads India's current coalition government. The Muslim lawyer did win the next election to the State Legislative Assembly as a BJP candidate.

7. State Legislative Assembly

8. The Reservation System has become one of the most important political issues in India. The upper castes hate it, but they cannot stop it without first destroying India's fledgling democracy.

9. As a result of the social engineering of the Reservation System,

the Congress Party had already lost the upper caste voters. Mummy attempted to pacify its upper caste base by insulting Dr. Maurya. In the process she lost the lower caste voters, the beneficiaries of her party's policies. The lawyer wanted to grab both the lower and the upper caste votes. The upper castes had already switched their political loyalty from Congress to BJP. If the lawyer could get me to stand up for the lower castes he would be able to take political credit from my actions.

10. Like *Jatavs*, the *Chamars* are leather-workers, members of the Scheduled Castes and untouchables. In many northern states of India they have become one of the most powerful political forces.

11. In most places in India the District Collector, the revenue officer, also serves as the District Magistrate – the chief law enforcement officer.

12. See Gene Edward Veith's book *Fascism: Modern and Postmodern* (Nivedit Good Books, Mussoorie, India, 2000) p. 126.

13. There is no other way to understand why the defenders of Hinduism who are using force to persecute Christians and to reconvert Christians to Hinduism keep repeating a blatant lie that Christians use force to convert Hindus. I myself was arrested on a trumped up case of using force in an attempt to convert. The charge was that, along with four others, I held a revolver at a Hindu's head to force him to convert. It took three years for the court to dismiss the case on the ground that three Hindus and a Muslim could not possibly have helped me in such a crime. Can such morally bankrupt people really succeed in defending an obviously immoral religious system?

14. The Holy Bible – Matthew 22:39

15. Photocopiers were not available in the district at that time.

16. The ancient Hindu lawgiver

17. A Brahmin lawyer, who opposed me for years before becoming a good friend

18. The Holy Bible – Luke 4:18-19

19. The Holy Bible – Isaiah 58:6-12

20. The Holy Bible – John 4:4-42

21. The Holy Bible – Matthew 9:9-13

22. The Holy Bible – Matthew 8:1-4

23. The Holy Bible – Matthew 8:5-11 (see also Acts 10 & 11)

24. The Holy Bible – Matthew 5:43-47

25. The Holy Bible – John 8:31-32

26. The Holy Bible – John 8:34, 36

27. It is for this reason I have never been a part of "Dalit Theology," which appears to me to be built on a spirituality of hatred, camouflaged as "justice."

Chapter 2: Manju's Honour

1. Scheduled Caste

2. Tenth standard/grade

3. The highest category of academic grade, usually over 60%

4. Usually over 75%

5. A major Scheduled Caste of leather-workers

6. "The fruit of patience is sweet."

7. Other Backward Castes

8. Hand-rolled cigarettes made with the tobacco inside a *tendu* leaf

9. Land-owning ruling caste Rajputs

10. A large plate

11. Social etiquette

12. Stone mansion with high walls and a courtyard

13. Farewell ceremony to conclude wedding celebrations

14. Ruffians, petty gangsters
15. Fishermen
16. Member of Parliament
17. Followers of Indian socialist leader Ram Manohar Lohia
18. The lower chamber of the Indian Parliament made up of directly elected representatives
19. The Holy Bible – Matthew 20:25-28; Mark 10:42-45
20. Hindi formula films that flood out of the world's most prolific production centre, Bombay (Mumbai)
21. Errand boy
22. Etiquette
23. India's corruption
24. University Grants Commission
25. The Holy Bible – Ephesians 5:25
26. The Holy Bible – Matthew 19:4-6

Chapter 3: A Temple in the River

1. The Holy Bible: Proverbs 3:19-20; Proverbs 24:3-4; Ecclesiastes 2:26
2. The Holy Bible – Exodus 20:2-3
3. The Holy Bible – Colossians 1:16
4. The Holy Bible – Romans 3:23; see also Isaiah 6:3,5; Revelation 4:8.
5. The Holy Bible – John 16:7-11
6. The Holy Bible – 1 John 4:16
7. The Holy Bible – John 3:16
8. The Holy Bible – Genesis 1:27; Genesis 5:1
9. See *Death of a Guru* by Rabi R. Maharaj (OM Books, Secunderabad, India, 1998).
10. Givers

11. Takers

12. The Holy Bible – Matthew 8:28-34

13. The Holy Bible – Matthew 10:1

14. The Holy Bible – Matthew 28:18-19

15. See, for example, my book *Truth and Social Reform* (Nivedit Good Books, Mussoorie, India, 1996).

16. The Holy Bible – Genesis 1:28

17. The Holy Bible – Psalm 24:1, Psalm 50:12, Psalm 89:1, 1 Corinthians 10:26

18. See The Holy Bible – Genesis 2 & 3

19. The Holy Bible – Revelation 11:18

20. See Jotiba Phule's book *Priest-craft Exposed* in *Collected Works of Mahatma Jotiba Phule* Vol. II (Bombay: Education Department, Govt. of Maharashtra, 1991).

21. For further discussion of this point see my fourth letter to Arun Shourie in *Missionary Conspiracy: Letters To A Postmodern Hindu* (Nivedit Good Books, Mussoorie, India, 1996 & 1998).

22. The Holy Bible – John 4:24

23. The Holy Bible – Genesis 1:26-27

24. The Holy Bible – Matthew 22:37-40; James 2:8-9-12 and 1 John 4:20-21

25. The Holy Bible – Psalms 24:1

26. The Holy Bible – Deuteronomy 4:9-10; Psalm 34:11; Psalm 78:5

27. The Holy Bible – Isaiah 33:22; Psalm 96:13; Acts 17:31

28. See the following for an understanding of Magna Carta:
The Avalon Project at the Yale Law School, "Documents in Law, History and Diplomacy" http://www.yale.edu/lawweb/avalon/avalon.htm

Howard, A. E. Dick *Magna Carta : Text and Commentary* Revised edition (1997) University Press of Virginia; ISBN: 0813901219

Holt, James C. *Magna Carta* 2nd edition (1992) Cambridge University Press (Pap Txt); ISBN: 0521277787.

29. *"I, ABC, do swear in the name of God / solemnly affirm that I will faithfully execute the office of President (or discharge the function of the President) of India and will to the best of my ability preserve, protect and defend the Constitution and the law and that I will devote myself to the service and well-being of the people of India."* Constitution of India, Article 60, Oath or affirmation by the President of India.

30. Bevere, John, *The Fear of the Lord*: Discover the Key to Intimately Knowing God (1997) Creation House; ISBN: 0884194868

Bridges, Jerry *The Joy of Fearing God* (1998) Waterbrook Press; ISBN: 1578560292

Dawson, Joy, *Intimate Friendship With God Through Understanding The Fear Of The Lord* (1986) Chosen Books; ISBN: 0800790847

Kistler Don (Ed), Bunyan, John A.; *The Fear of God* (1999) Soli Deo Gloria Publications; ISBN: 1573580848

31. The Holy Bible – Ephesians 2:10

32. Matthew 24:14-30; Luke 19:11-27

33. Ball, William Bentley, *What's A Constitution Without Natural Law?* in The Laws of Nature and of Nature's God 5, Plymouth Rock Foundation Inc. ed. (1992)

Barton, David, *Original Intent: The Courts, the Constitution, and Religion* 2nd edition (1997) Wallbuilder Press; ISBN: 0925279579

Gerhart, Eugene C. *American Liberty and "Natural Law"*, The Beacon Press, Boston; (1986) Fred B Rothman & Co; ISBN: 0837722063

Eidsmoe, John *Christianity and the Constitution: The Faith of Our*

Founding Fathers (June 1995) Baker Book House; ISBN: 0801052319

34. The Holy Bible – Genesis 1:26-27
35. *Purushasukta* creation hymn in *Rig Veda*
36. The Holy Bible – Genesis 3:20
37. The Holy Bible – John 3:16, see also 1 John 4:16
38. The Holy Bible – John 1:11-12
39. The Holy Bible – John 3:3-6
40. The Holy Bible – Acts 2:38
41. The Holy Bible – Revelation 1:6
42. The Holy Bible – 1 Peter 2:9
43. The Holy Bible – Revelation 3:4; John 14:1-3
44. The Holy Bible – John 4:7
45. The Holy Bible – Matthew 9:9-13
46. The Holy Bible – Matthew 8:1-4
47. The Holy Bible – Matthew 8:5-13
48. The Holy Bible – Luke 7:36-50
49. The Holy Bible – Matthew 9:20-22
50. The Holy Bible – Matthew 28:19
51. The Holy Bible – Acts 10, 11 & Galatians 2:11-13
52. The Holy Bible – Galatians 2:14-21
53. The Holy Bible – Acts 15 and Galatians 2:1-10
54. The Holy Bible – Acts 11:19-26
55. The Holy Bible – Revelation 7:9

Chapter 4: The Leper

1. Potboiler formula films from India's celluloid capital, Bombay (Mumbai)
2. Idol worship
3. Member of Legislative Assembly of their state

Chapter 5: Where Should Satish Go?

1. A bracelet tied by sisters at an annual festival to affirm their brothers' protection of them
2. *Bhangi* or *Valmiki* is the sweeper caste, the lowest of the low. Because they handled garbage and (traditionally) "nightsoil" (human waste) they were considered extremely "polluting" and hence "untouchable."
3. The leather-worker caste. Because they traditionally handled hides of dead animals they too were considered "polluting" and therefore "untouchable."
4. An asylum, a place of refuge, a charitable shelter

Chapter 6: Conversion as Revolution

1. Before dividing India into States or Provinces for administrative purposes, the British had divided it into Presidencies.
2. On October 13, 1935, at a conference at Nasik, Dr. Ambedkar reviewed the progress made on the condition of the "untouchables" in the decade since he had started his agitation. Ambedkar declared that their efforts had not borne the kind of results he had expected. He then made his dramatic appeal to all "untouchables," encouraging them to forsake the Hindu religion and convert to a religion where they would be treated with equality.

3. *Jatibhed Ka Uchhed* by B. R. Ambedkar (Bahujan Kalyan Prakashan, Lucknow, 1986) originally published in English in 1936.

4. Charles Grant and William Carey are the true parents of "modern" India, Pakistan and Bangladesh. Their work was the basis for all the efforts of Raja Ram Mohun Roy, Lord Macaulay, Jotiba Phule, Mahatma Gandhi, Dr. Ambedkar, Mohammad Ali Jinnah and Jawaharlal Nehru to change India. For a fuller discussion of Grant's role see my books *Missionary Conspiracy: Letters to a Postmodern Hindu* and *India: The Grand Experiment*. (Available from Orders@SouthAsianResources.com)

5. Grant's 1786 Proposal is reproduced in the fifth chapter of my book *Missionary Conspiracy: Letters to a Postmodern Hindu*. Six years later Grant developed his proposal into a book, *Observations on the State of Society among the Asiatic Subjects of Great Britain, particularly with respect to Morals and on the Means of Improving it. Written Chiefly in the Year 1792.* The handwritten version of this treatise was circulated to Members of Parliament in 1792 to try and shape the East India Company's Charter, which was to be renewed by the British Parliament in 1793. The book was privately published in 1797. Eventually, in 1812, it was published as a State paper, by order of the British Parliament. It shaped the Charters of 1813, 1833, and 1853. His book is extensively quoted in the official records of the Government of India, see, *Selections From The Educational Records*, New Delhi, National Archives of India, pp 81-90.

6. Wesley – the founder of Methodism – was the human force behind the eighteenth century spiritual revival that made England the greatest nation on earth between the eighteenth and twentieth centuries. For a fuller treatment of this subject see the chapter "Matrix of Missions: The Wesleyan

Revival" in my book *Missionary Conspiracy: Letters To A Postmodern Hindu.*

7. Although Martin Luther had begun the process of involving aristocracy and merchants in financing education in Protestant countries, education was still a ministry of the Church in Grant's day, not of the state. European universities grew out of monasteries and cathedral schools, and most teachers were "Reverends," licensed by Bishops.

8. William Carey had entered India "illegally" as a missionary in spite of the East India Company's prohibitions. That is why he lived in Serampore – a Danish, not British, territory.

9. Widow burning. For details see *The Legacy of William Carey* by Vishal and Ruth Mangalwadi (Crossway Books, Wheaton, Illinois, 1999).

10. The Holy Bible – Matthew 22:37-40

11. The Holy Bible – Luke 19:10

12. David Landes, *The Wealth and Poverty of Nations: Why Some Are So Rich And Some So Poor,* (W. W. Norton & Co., New York, 1998) pp. 133-135

13. Ibid p. 32

14. Quoted by Stephen McDowell, *Providential Perspective,* Vol. 10, No. 3, June 1995.

15. John Acton, *The History of Freedom*, (The Acton Institute, 1993) p. 23

16. Gertrude Himmwelfarb, *Lord Acton: A Study In Conscience and Politics* (ICS Press, 1993) p. 134

17. The Holy Bible – John 8:32

18. See Jotirao Phule's *Slavery (In the Civilised British Government Under the Cloak of Brahaminism)* by Keer and Malshe [eds] in *Collected Works of Jotirao Phule* (Education Department, Government of Maharashtra, Bombay, 1991), and *Caste, Conflict and Ideology* by

Rosalind O'Hanlon (Cambridge University Press, Cambridge, 1985)

19. Quoted by Stephen McDowell, *Providential Perspective*, Vol. 10, No. 3, June 1995.

20. Quoted by Veith in *Fascism – Modern and Postmodern* (Nivedit Good Books, Mussoorie, India, 2000) p.126. Hitler was wrong as far as the human experience is concerned. All human beings have a moral conscience, however weak or poorly developed it may be. However, Hitler was right in that the human conscience made logical sense only in the context of Jewish monotheism. David Gress observes, "The Israelites thus contributed monotheism to the West. This contribution was important not as a religion or theology, but because monotheism made a radical distinction between the divine and the human. This distinction had two consequences. It emphasized the moral value of individual human acts and thus helped to create the idea of an individual conscience and individual responsibility [and consequently of individual rights]. Second, it directed human attention to understanding nature, both human and nonhuman, and this impulse. . .made possible science and democracy." (*From Plato to Nato*, The Free Press, New York, 1998, p. 41)

21. Veith. p.125

22. "Secular" and "humanism" are positive terms in India. "Secular" is usually used as the anti-thesis of "communal" and "humanism" is used as a synonym for "humanitarianism." In the West, however, the phrase "secular humanism" has come to mean a man-centered, God-denying belief system.

23. The Holy Bible – Proverbs 2

24. Quoted in *Liberating the Nations*, by Stephen McDowell and Mark Beliles (Providence Foundation, Charlottesville, VA, 1995) p. 11-12.

25. For a fuller discussion of this point, please see my book, *India: The Grand Experiment*.

26. This subject has been discussed at length in my book, *India: The Grand Experiment*.

27. Literally: "Insistence on truth." A Gandhian term for the struggle for reform through passive resistance.

28. Jainism was allowed to exist, but only because it accommodated itself to Hinduism to the point that it was not a threat. Sikhism was born after Islam had weakened the political power of the Hindus. And it has survived by compromising with the caste-system. To say that Hindu India had never known freedom is not to claim that it was completely static culture. In as much as human beings are inherently creative, no culture can be completely static, however much it may try to suppress freedom. There was plenty of creative dynamism in the Indian culture. My point is that, as a rule, Hindu culture has always suppressed, not supported free-dom.

29. See the appendix, "From New Physics to Hinduism" in my book, *When The New Age Gets Old: Looking For A Greater Spirituality*, (IVP, Downers Grove, IL, 1992).

30. Acts 17:29-31

31. ©Gloria & William J. Gaither

32. For a discussion of Rationalism, Mysticism, and Revelation, please see my third Letter to Mr. Arun Shourie, entitled, "Postmodern Indians – Following A Western Folly" in *Missionary Conspiracy: Letters to A Postmodern Hindu*, (Nivedit Good Books, Mussoorie, India, 1998).

33. For example see the section, "England Before and After Wesley" in Letter Eight in my book, *Missionary Conspiracy: Letters To A Postmodern Hindu*.

34. The "Orthodox churches" are one of the three branches of Chris-

tianity, the others being the Roman Catholic and the Protestant. The Orthodox do not accept the authority of the Pope, which the Roman Catholics came to accept much later in history. In contrast to the Orthodox and the Roman Catholics, Protestants (who are so called because they "protested" against corruption in the Roman Catholic Church) wish to continuously test tradition as well as new ideas by the teachings of the Bible. In theory, the Orthodox and the Roman Catholics also accept the authority of the Bible; however, they accord the Bible a lesser place than their traditions. Protestants are of various different denominations (Anglicans, Methodists, Baptists, Lutherans, Mennonites, Presbyterians, Pentecostals, and so on) but these differences are marginal and arose out of the fact that the protests against Roman Catholicism were started by different individuals, in different languages, within different cultures, and at different times. Some modern Protestants have started subordinating the Bible to the intellectual fashions of our time. Those who reject such fashions and continue to submit themselves to the authority of the Bible are called Evangelicals or Biblical Christians. Confusingly, but encouragingly, many who are members of the Roman Catholic and Orthodox Churches, have now rejected the supremacy of their tradition and of the Pope and accept the supremacy of the Bible, so these people are in fact Evangelicals or Biblical Christians even though they continue in their own churches.

35. Nancy, the Professor's wife – an American – who teaches Art History at the University of Moscow, added that the moral standards in America that her husband had described were rapidly fading as Bill Clinton's generation had turned its back on the Christian faith. Nevertheless, her husband's observations regarding the cause of the different moral standards in the two countries were valid.

36. The Holy Bible – Revelation 20:11-15

Chapter 7: Two Enlightenments and One Light

1. The Holy Bible – John 16:33

2. The Holy Bible – John 1:4, 9

3. A. L. Basham, "*The Wonder That Was India.*" (Rupa & Co., New Delhi, 2000, Third Revised Edition) p. 269

4 The Holy Bible – John 10:10

5 See *How Should We Then Live: Rise and Decline of Western Thought and Culture* by Francis A. Schaeffer (Good News Publishers, 1983; ISBN: 0891072926); *How Now Shall We Live?* by Charles W. Colson, Nancy Pearcey (Tyndale House Publishers, 1999; ISBN: 0842318089); and the author's forthcoming book and documentary series *"The Book of the Millennium: How The Bible Changed Civilization"* (working title, anticipated release 2003).

6. *Rise and Fall of the Third Reich : A History of Nazi Germany* Shirer, William L. (1991 Fawcett Publications, ISBN: 0449219771); *Adolf Hitler* Toland, John Reissue Edition (1992 Anchor Books/ Doubleday, ISBN: 0385420536); *Mussolini,* Ridley, Jasper (1998, St. Martins Press ISBN: 0312193033); *The Black Book of Communism: Crimes, Terror, Repression,* Courtois, Stephane et al. (1999 Harvard University Press, ISBN: 0674076087)

7. Gnosticism refers to the thought and practice, particularly of various Asian and European cults of the late pre-Christian and early Christian centuries, distinguished by the conviction that matter is evil and that liberation comes through "gnosis" or esoteric spiritual wisdom. The *Upanishads* are the last of the Vedic literature written as philosophic discourses by the hermit gurus before the Christian era.

8. A. L. Basham, *op. cit.* pp. 269-270

9. Not all forms of Christianity have produced identical social

and intellectual fruits. Emphasis on rationality and creativity developed in that part of the church which was closer to a Biblical worldview.

10. In Judeo/Christian meditation, God commands positive meditation on himself, his law and his acts. See Joshua 1:7-8; Psalm 1:1-2. "Transcendental" meditation seeks to blank the mind and focus on nothing.

11. A related question is: Why did Christian civilization succeed in halting both Islamic and Communist expansion in the West as well as in the East? Many Indians forget that it was Christian England that liberated India from Islam.

12. The Holy Bible – John 1:1, 2, 14; Proverbs 8:22-31

13. The Holy Bible – Colossians 2:3

14. The Holy Bible – Colossians 1:15

15. The Holy Bible – Genesis 1:26-27; 5:1-2; 9:6

16. For a detailed discussion see the appendix "From New Physics to Hinduism" in my book, *When The New Age Gets Old: Looking For A Greater Spirituality* (IVP, Downers Grove, IL, 1992). This appendix is available on the internet, at www.Karma2Grace.org.

17. See *Escape From Reason* by Francis A. Schaeffer, in *Complete Works of Francis A. Schaeffer* (Crossway Books, Wheaton, Illinois, 1985; ISBN: 0891073310).

18. See the following chapter and the book, *William Carey and the Regeneration of India* by Ruth & Vishal Mangalwadi (Nivedit Good Books, Mussoorie, India, 1997) or *Legacy of William Carey: A Model for the Transformation of a Culture* by Vishal and Ruth Mangalwadi (Crossway Books, Wheaton, Illinois, 1999; ISBN:1581341121).

19. A good study of Christianity's formative influence on Phule and the origin of the Dalit revolt is *Caste, Conflict, and Ideology* by Rosalind O' Hanlin (Cambridge University Press, Cambridge, 1985). English translations of Phule's own works have been published by the Education Department of the Government of Maharashtra. See,

for example, *Collected Works of Mahatma Jotiba Phule* Vols. I & II (1991).

20. Mahatma Phule is mistaken here, as the English had no contact with the Greeks before Christ and the Greek language was not taught in England until the sixteenth century AD.

21. *Slavery: Collected Works of Mahatma Jotirao Phule,* Vol I. (Translated by Prof. P. G. Patil) Education Department, Government of Maharashtra, 1991, pp. 58-59

22. *Rajashree Sahu Gaurav Granth,* Edited by P. B. Salukke Kolhapuri. (Maharashtra Rajya Shikshan Vibhag, Sachivalaya, Bombay) pp. 451-452

23. Most followers of Kanshiram are now interested in personal political power rather than India's social transformation.

24. Literally "majority community" — a reference to the fact that the "lower castes" together with India's minorities constitute the majority of India's population

25. *Indian Development: Selected Regional Perspectives,* Edited by Jean Dreze & Amartya Sen (Oxford University Press, Delhi, 1997) p. 15-16

26. Brahminism begins with a falsehood that a given caste is born superior.

27. *Selections: Collected Works of Mahatma Jotirao Phule* Vol. II, p.121

28. Ibid.

29. See his novel, *The Untouchable.*

30. Western universities grew out of Catholic monasteries and Cathedral schools. The Protestant Pietists set up the first "modern" university in Halle, inspired by the works of John Amos Comenius.

31. Incarnation

32. Court, especially in the context of the Moghuls; in this context, the ministers of the Government of India and others dignitaries in the capital city

33. The Holy Bible — John 14:6

Chapter 9: Has India Died ?

1. India's current government is a coalition called the National Democratic Alliance (NDA), which is led by the Bhartiya Janata Party (BJP).
2. The Hindu fascist ideology whose political face is the BJP.
3. The Holy Bible – Ezekiel 37:3
4. Although the Old Testament prophets Elijah and Elisha had miraculously raised some from the dead, the belief in resurrection became common only after Christ's resurrection. Over 500 people saw the risen Lord Jesus Christ.

Afterword: The Shadow of the Untouchable

1. John 3:16
2. Porter
3. Light one-horse two-wheeled buggy or carriage
4. The gatekeeper
5. Now Bangladesh
6. J. W. Pickett, *Christ's Way To India's Heart*, (Lucknow Publishing House, Lucknow, 1938 & 1960) p. 22
7. 3 million